IT'S ALL TRASH 'TIL IT'S CASH

APPLYING AMAZON'S BLUEPRINT FOR BUILDERS

Chadd SJ Ciccarelli

For permission requests, write to the publisher at contact@identitypublications.com.

Library of Congress Control Number: 2025905458

Orders by U.S. trade bookstores and wholesalers. Please contact Identity Publications: Tel: (805) 259-3724 or visit www.IdentityPublications.com.

ISBN-13: 978-1-945884-73-3 (ebook)
ISBN-13: 978-1-945884-89-4 (paperback)
ISBN-13: 978-1-945884-88-7 (hardcover)

First Edition, published in Buffalo, Wyoming, by Identity Publications. (www.IdentityPublications.com).

DEDICATION

You've heard me say it before—*"It's all trash 'til it's cash."* That was my go-to response anytime someone floated big leadership dreams or poked around in my sales pipeline. But the truth is, none of it—the wins, the losses, the lessons—happened in a vacuum. Behind every deal closed and every project launched was a crew of misfits, overachievers, and sharp minds who made the madness not just bearable but worthwhile.

To all my Amazon colleagues, past and present—this journey was forged in the trenches with you. The late nights, the impossible deadlines, the battles we fought, and the wins we barely paused to celebrate—these stories are as much yours as they are mine.

This book isn't just a collection of those stories—it's a blueprint. The lessons learned, the scars earned, and the truths uncovered are here for you to apply to your business, your hustle, your next big move. Here's to the relentless grind, the unfiltered truths, and the memories we forged in the fire.

CONTENTS

ACKNOWLEDGMENTS

Before you dive in, let's be clear: This isn't a gossip column. While the stories are real, I've kept names out. Any name you see is fabricated. The goal here isn't to name-drop but to capture the essence of mastering interviewing and hiring in a challenging world. Focus on the lessons, not the names.

PREFACE

Life, leadership, and entrepreneurship often feel like rummaging through piles of chaos, searching for that one gem that can change everything. The title *It's All Trash 'til It's Cash* encapsulates a fundamental truth: value isn't inherent—it's created. Leadership, like the alchemy of turning trash into treasure, requires vision, resilience, and the courage to navigate ambiguity.

This book is an exploration of that transformation. Each chapter is a thread in the larger tapestry of leadership, innovation, and cultural adaptation. From balancing individuality with a cohesive vision to navigating interviews that strip away fluff and uncover substance, every lesson reflects the intricate dance of turning potential into impact.

The journey of leadership is about balancing culture and individuality, risk and opportunity, vision and execution. Like Darwin's observations on survival, it's not about being the strongest or smartest but about adaptability, responsiveness, and the relentless pursuit of growth. Whether you're leading a team, scaling a startup, or navigating the global stage, the principles shared here reveal how to turn the raw material of ideas into tangible, meaningful results.

In leadership, nothing begins as gold. But with enough grit, clarity, and intentionality, what might first appear as trash can transform into something extraordinary.

INTRODUCTION

I wrote this book because I had the unique experience of being part of Amazon during a time when it wasn't the tech giant it is today. In 2010, Yahoo was still dominant, and Amazon's advertising arm was virtually nonexistent. But by 2011, I joined the company—on Valentine's Day, no less—when the ad team was completely new. At the time, it was hard to imagine that advertising would eventually become one of Amazon's biggest revenue streams, comparable to A.

What compelled me to share my story was the journey I went on during my twelve-and-a-half years in this unique environment and the unconventional lessons learned behind the scenes. In many ways, working with Amazon during its early days was like earning a PhD in business. More than just the technical side of things, it was also about navigating the internal politics. In a place like Amazon, having the best idea wasn't always enough. You had to be strategic, network well, and understand the importance of playing politics. Otherwise, even the most innovative ideas wouldn't gain traction.

Over the years, I learned a lot about leadership, company culture, and the subtle dynamics that could make or break projects. Many people don't realize that leadership can change the entire trajectory of a company, and culture can either sustain or derail progress. One of the best pieces of advice I ever received came from my colleague, Tomo, who shared some wisdom during my first management role at Lending Tree, where I worked years before joining Amazon. He looked at me one day and said, "Chadd, you're managing people now. I know you love football. So, will your team be the Dallas Cowboys or the Pittsburgh Steelers? What's your leadership style? Remember, a team is a reflection of its leader. Never forget that."

It hit me then, and it's echoed ever since—even in words from Jeff Bezos, who talked about culture the same way. If people are falling short, burning out, or walking away, that's not a people problem—that's a leadership problem. You don't build a team by luck or by chance. You shape it, and in the process, it shapes you right back and you need to have some guidelines and a philosophy in place.

Being there for over a decade made me an outlier—very few people last more than two years at Amazon. That longevity gave me a front-row seat to the pressures that come with balancing mental health in a high-pressure environment like that. I saw first-hand how leadership and mental resilience can affect one's career, especially in an environment where rapid expansion, international growth, and constant change were the norms.

This book is not just about my time at Amazon; it's about sharing what I learned and how those lessons can be applied to both startups and established corporations. I contend that the lessons I learned are more valuable than an MBA in many ways. I wasn't a business major; I studied Philosophy at Carnegie Mellon. But my time at Amazon taught me more about executing ideas, managing teams, and navigating the complexities of corporate culture than any classroom ever could.

The most important takeaway from my experience, and what you'll learn more about in the pages that follow, is understanding how to take calculated risks, fail fast, and pivot when necessary. Amazon had a culture of encouraging big thinking and rewarding those who weren't afraid to take risks, even if they sometimes failed. But they also had a deep focus on data-driven decision-making. You had to understand your inputs—how many calls you needed to make, your conversion rates, and all the nuts and bolts that would ultimately drive your success. The output would only follow if you understood the inputs, and this philosophy became ingrained in everything I did, from working on groundbreaking programs to recovering from failures like the infamous Fire Phone.

Ultimately, this book is for anyone who wants to learn how to take an idea from nothing and turn it into something. It's about the importance of leadership, resilience, and adaptability in the modern business landscape. My goal is to offer readers a crash course in business strategy, the Amazon way of working, and the lessons that I believe are applicable far beyond the walls of one company.

BACKGROUND

San Francisco in 2010 was a beast of restless energy, a city where dreams were spun from tech ambitions and the fog rolled in like whispered secrets. Amidst the sprawling cable cars and the relentless buzz of innovation, I found myself itching for a change. The lure of Los Angeles called to me—not for its promise of fame or the shimmer of Hollywood lights, but for something more grounded, something that resonated with a different kind of ambition, and I was simply more LA than SF.

My story with Amazon began not in the gleaming offices of a tech giant, but in the less glamorous corridors of Adzinia. Back then, Amazon was not considered Silicon Valley, the disruptor everyone clamored to be associated with. It was more of a shadow player, staying under and always minimizing its tax exposure across its sprawling empire. In fact, in those days, you could order from Amazon and not pay any sales tax, which was about 7.25% in 2010. Adzinia, which you now know as Amazon Advertising, was this new "thing" that the Retail team did not really like, originally christened Adzinia—a name that sounds almost as enigmatic as the strategies employed behind closed doors.

Living in San Francisco, surrounded by the relentless pace of startups and the ever-present scent of ambition, I felt a pull toward Los Angeles. It wasn't the tech scene that beckoned me; it was the opportunity to be part of something meticulously crafted, something that operated on a different wavelength. At that time, Amazon was far from the tech darling it would become, but to me, that was exactly the intrigue I needed.

One evening, I stumbled upon a job posting on LinkedIn:

JOB DESCRIPTION

Sales Account Executive, Online Advertising

Adzinia, an Amazon company, is currently seeking ambitious Sales Executives to develop and grow its successful Global Online Display Advertising business. We are leveraging world-class personalization technologies, broad reach, and brand affiliation to offer advertising solutions to a select group of top-tier brands. The Sales Executive will be responsible for generating revenue by negotiating a broad range of advertising deals. This self-motivated individual will cultivate deep relationships with people at both senior and tactical levels of Fortune 500 companies and ad agencies and should have a strong client and agency Rolodex.

Our ideal candidate will have at least seven years of total sales experience and a minimum of 3-5 years of online sales experience at a major Web property. A consultative selling style is desired, coupled with the structure and organizational skills needed to drive deals to closure in a new business environment. Candidates must feel comfortable prospecting, cold-calling, and negotiating in person and via phone on both transactional and high-value/exposure deals. Additionally, the ability to identify, develop, and manage a valuable prospect list based on our standard product offerings is crucial.

Requirements:

◈ 3-5 years of relevant online advertising sales experience

◈ 7+ years of total sales experience

◈ Demonstrated ability to consistently close sales and generate revenues

◈ Strong track record of high-level negotiation and successful internal and external relationship management

◈ Strong analytical abilities

◈ Ability to interact with a broad set of businesses and presenting both over the phone and in person

❖ Excellent written and verbal communication skills, strong attention to detail, and good follow-through
❖ Bachelor's degree required
❖ Entertainment Industry Experience
❖ Interest in Entertainment
❖ Interest in Consumer Electronics
❖ Consumer Electronics Industry Experience

The words jumped off the screen, each requirement a testament to the rigor and precision that Adzinia—Amazon in its more unassuming avatar—demanded. This wasn't just another sales job; it was a doorway into a world where data met creativity, where algorithms danced with human intuition.

Applying felt like stepping into the unknown. Amazon's reputation for playing the long game was well-earned; their mastery in leveraging every available rule and law to minimize tax obligations across its myriad businesses was almost an art form. Adzinia, as a part of this colossal machine, operated with a similar finesse. It wasn't just about selling advertising space; it was about understanding the intricate ballet of global markets, personalization technologies, and brand dynamics.

I reached out to the recruiter, a gatekeeper who seemed to understand the labyrinthine nature of Adzinia's hiring process. Coordinating with her was like navigating a diplomatic mission—carefully timed emails, precise scheduling, and the ever-present undercurrent of anticipation. Soon enough, I found myself on a plane from San Francisco to Seattle, the heart of Amazon's operations, embarking on what felt like an odyssey into corporate America's hidden trenches.

Seattle was a different beast altogether. The city was drenched in rain, its skyline a silhouette against a perpetually gray sky. The Amazon campus sprawled before me as I had my interviews at the Wainwright Building, named after the first Amazon customer, an impressive testament to the company's growing might. Inside, the air was thick with ambition and the quiet hum of relentless productivity. My days were packed with a merciless onslaught of meetings—each one peeling back another layer of Adzinia's intricate machinery.

I met with various people, each interaction a piece of the puzzle that was the "new" ads business. There were strategists who spoke in acronyms and analysts who could parse data like poets reciting verses. It was a relentless barrage, testing not just my sales acumen but my ability to adapt and thrive in an environment that thrived on chaos and precision in equal measure.

The pivotal moment came during a meeting with the hiring manager, Elisabeth, a sharp-eyed veteran who seemed to see right through me but was also very warm and welcoming. Her questions were incisive, each one designed to uncover not just my skills but my very essence as a salesperson. But it wasn't just her I had to impress. There was the bar raiser—a role as enigmatic as its name suggested—whose sole purpose was to ensure that only the best joined their ranks. This process included another person shadowing the bar raiser, adding another layer of scrutiny. It was a split decision, a balancing act between proving my worth and aligning with Amazon's lofty standards, all while grappling with my own lack of experience at the time.

After returning to San Francisco, I was hit with the news that I had to do one more interview. By then, I'd already navigated through eight interviews, each one more intense than the last. The final hurdle was an interview with the VP of the business, located back in Oakland by the Clorox building—a figure who embodied the company's strategic vision. This was my last chance to make an impression, to show that I wasn't just another cog in the sales machine but a force to be reckoned with.

I received an email from Lisa, the coordinator, detailing the next steps, which included a breakfast with the VP, also named Lisa.

On the morning of the interview, I walked into the Marriott Oakland City Center with a mix of optimism and anxiety. The lobby was sleek, a stark contrast to the chaotic mall office in Sherman Oaks where my first day had been a debacle. This was the real deal, the final gate before either being swallowed by Amazon's vast machinery or finding myself back on the streets of San Francisco.

As I entered the meeting room, the VP stood to greet me, embodying the strategic vision I had to align with. This was my last chance to make an impression, to demonstrate that I wasn't just another player but a standout talent. In a move that harkened back to old-school salesmanship, I pulled out my paystub and slammed it onto the table. It was a bold, almost reckless gesture, one that could have backfired spectacularly. But I was confident, and that was my way of merging into audacity. I wasn't looking for the role because I was desperate—I was looking to show that I had nothing to lose and everything to offer. And it worked. The paystub was more than just a piece of paper; it was a testament to my ability to close deals to generate revenue as my commission was broken out to show that I was the best at what I did. The VP loved it, and I was hired and greeted with her colleague who was also a director at the time, Zakk.

A few days later, the official offer was made: a Los Angeles-based role, and Amazon paid for my relocation from San Francisco to Los Angeles. It was a twist I hadn't anticipated but one that underscored the company's intricate web of operations. My first day was slated for Valentine's Day, a day symbolic of beginnings and connections, but it started on a rocky note.

The Amazon office, or more specifically, the IMDb office, was nestled in the Sherman Oaks Galleria. If you've ever been to a mall that reeks of pure cliché commerce—think PF Chang's, Cheesecake Factory, and Paul Mitchell The School Sherman Oaks —then you have a sense of where this was. It was arguably the lamest mall in America, a hub where the sheen of consumerism met the banalities of suburban shopping.

I arrived late for my first day—why, you ask? Because navigating the Sherman Oaks Galleria felt like trekking through a labyrinth of consumerist mediocrity. The office lacked the sleek signage or a clear directory, making the search feel like an initiation into obscurity. After wandering aimlessly, I managed to reach the office administrator, Paige. Her presence was a beacon in the maze of mall stores, and she came down to find me. I was relieved yet apprehensive. First impressions are everything, and I couldn't afford to start on the wrong foot.

"Why don't you have any signs on the door or directory of the building?" I asked Paige, trying to mask my frustration with a veneer of casual inquiry.

She sighed, a mixture of irritation and resignation in her voice. "All the people that work at the Sherman Oaks Galleria come up demanding credit for speaking roles to get their SAG[1] cards." This now makes a lot of sense as to why no sign was posted because that was the ultimate milestone for any struggling actor.

It was a bizarre explanation, one that hinted at the quirky, almost surreal environment I was now a part of. But it also underscored the peculiar challenges of integrating into Amazon's expansive yet compartmentalized operations. My journey to starting at Amazon was anything but straightforward—a reflection of the company itself, complex and multifaceted.

Leaving San Francisco was more than a geographical shift; it was an escape from the relentless grind and the personal setbacks that had plagued me. My car had been broken into for the fourth time, each incident eroding my sense of security and pushing me closer to the idea of returning to Los Angeles. The city's sprawling landscapes and diverse industries offered a different kind of canvas—one where Adzinia could paint its strategies with broader strokes, away from the tech-centric chaos of San Francisco.

As I settled into my new role, the reality of Adzinia's operations became clear. It wasn't just about minimizing taxes or maximizing revenue; it was about understanding the intricate dance of global markets, about forging relationships

---

1   A **SAG Card** signifies membership in **SAG-AFTRA**, granting actors access to union-protected roles and benefits. **IMDb credits** help verify professional work, supporting eligibility for SAG membership.

that transcended mere transactions, and about building a business that could stand the test of time in an ever-evolving digital landscape while optimizing all of the custom data Amazon has accumulated. Los Angeles provided the perfect backdrop for this endeavor, its undercurrents of creativity and entertainment fueling innovative advertising solutions.

Looking back, that journey from San Francisco to Los Angeles, was a pivotal chapter in my story. It was a dive into the heart of a corporation that operated with the precision of a well-crafted recipe—minus the food, of course. It was about the flavors of strategy, the spice of negotiation, and the enduring essence of ambition.

And so, the journey at Amazon began—not with the flash of Silicon Valley fame, but with the quiet determination of a city seeking its own rhythm and a man ready to navigate the unseen hustles of corporate mastery. This book strips away the hype and the bullshit surrounding Amazon, uncovering the real lessons beneath the surface. It's also my way of putting that philosophy degree to work, navigating the complexities and truths of both startups and established businesses.

CHAPTER 1

NETWORKING AND CREATING VALUE

> *"The only true wisdom is in knowing you know nothing."*
> *— Socrates*

*I*n the fast-paced world of technology, where industry giants loom large and the landscape shifts daily, one lesson stands out: True success comes from a combination of resilience, adaptability, and the courage to venture into the unknown. It's in those uncharted territories that personal and professional growth occurs.

I found myself at the precipice of such a journey. Amidst the cold winter, my phone buzzed with an unexpected message from Amazon. The weight of that moment was profound—not just because it was Amazon, a company that had already become a formidable force in the marketplace, but because I knew this would be no ordinary career step. I wasn't preparing for just another job interview; I was gearing up for a transformative experience that would challenge every fiber of my professional being.

When I joined Amazon in early 2011, the tech world was on the verge of a revolution. Companies like Uber and Facebook were beginning to redefine their industries. Uber was reimagining urban mobility, Facebook was shaping the

1

global digital landscape, and Twitter was proving that even in 140 characters, revolutions could spark. At the same time, the iPhone was rapidly evolving, blurring the lines between technology and science fiction. In the midst of all this innovation stood Amazon, not content with its dominance in retail but expanding into new frontiers like advertising.

I was about to embark on my own journey into this rapidly expanding world. To get there, I already navigated the "split loop," Amazon's intense interview process designed to separate those who could thrive in its ecosystem from those who couldn't.

Amazon was no ordinary company, and my entry wasn't an ordinary experience. It felt like a test of survival, navigating a two-day marathon of interviews that ended in Oakland, a whirlwind of uncertainty. Yet, I emerged not just as an employee but as someone who had truly bought into the Amazon way. Surrounded by brilliant minds and constantly innovating, I wasn't overshadowed—I was inspired. Each day felt like a TED Talk, pushing me to grow, adapt, and contribute my own ideas to Amazon's legacy.

One of Amazon's core principles is to be customer obsessed. This focus on the customer experience drives everything the company does, no matter its size. It's a principle that can be applied to businesses of all sizes. Amazon's "Andon Cord," for example, empowers customer service representatives to pull a product from the site if there are too many complaints, prioritizing customer trust over short-term profits.

Navigating Amazon internally, however, was equally challenging. With constant turnover and rapid growth, I quickly learned that adaptability was key. No one stayed in a role for more than 12 to 16 months, and the company's size and complexity required a unique approach to success.

To navigate this behemoth, I leaned heavily on my network. Networking became essential to understanding how to work cross-functionally with different teams, each motivated by their own KPIs. The key was finding where I could add value and aligning my efforts with the goals of others. This give-and-take approach helped build my network and ensured I was able to contribute to projects in meaningful ways.

In an environment as ambiguous as Amazon, it wasn't just about what I knew—it was about who I knew and how I leveraged those relationships to get things done. Networking was a survival strategy, allowing me to navigate the constant change and ambiguity that defined my time there.

WHAT I LEARNED

1. **BUILD GOODWILL BEFORE YOU ASK:** Networking is about building authentic relationships, not just transactions. Offer value and insights before you seek help. This approach will pay off when you need it most.

2. **EMBRACE THE UNKNOWN:** Success often comes from stepping into unfamiliar territory. My journey at Amazon was daunting, but by embracing the unknown and leveraging my network, I made a lasting impact.

3. **OPPORTUNITIES EXIST BEYOND JOBS:** Networking isn't just for advancing your career—it can open doors, solve problems, and provide support in ways you wouldn't

expect. A single connection can lead to game-changing opportunities.

4. **CREATING VALUE THROUGH NETWORKS:** Networking isn't about quantity; it's about creating meaningful, value-driven connections. During my time at Amazon, my consistent interactions with key leaders allowed me to pivot from Los Angeles to London when the opportunity arose. By staying proactive and offering value, I was remembered when new roles emerged. This is the essence of effective networking: Staying relevant and making an impact that ensures you're top of mind when the right opportunity arises.

5. **AVOID THE BIGGEST NETWORKING MISTAKE:** The biggest mistake in networking is only reaching out when you need something. Focus on creating value for others and building relationships long before you ask for anything. Trust and reciprocity will follow.

6. **MAINTAIN CUSTOMER FOCUS:** No matter the size of your business, focusing on the customer can lead to long-term success. Amazon's scale didn't dilute its customer-first ethos, and neither should yours.

7. **EMBRACE AMBIGUITY:** Ambiguity is a constant in fast-growing companies. To succeed, you need to adapt, think critically, and leverage your network to navigate the unknown.

CHAPTER 2

HIRING LESSONS AND NOT RECOGNIZING THE OPPORTUNITY UNTIL YOU ARE IN IT

"The preservation of health should be the first study of one who is of any worth to oneself."
— *René Descartes*

Curiosity is the driving force behind leadership. It's the relentless punk rock anthem in the background, urging leaders to never settle, always question, and forever chase the horizon of knowledge.

When I joined Amazon, it was still a company finding its footing. Far from the global giant we know today, the culture was experimental, fueled by curiosity and a willingness to embrace the unknown. Jeff Bezos was accessible, the stock price hovered around $180 before ascending to $2,447 and recalibrating for the 20-for-1 split in 2022, and the focus was on building something great rather than obsessing over financial metrics. At the time, the company's "day one" philosophy was the cornerstone of Amazon's culture—innovation, risk-taking, and relentless learning were expected, not optional.

In the heart of Los Angeles, a city where dreams often collide with reality, the IMDb office at the Sherman Oaks Galleria became a hub of ambition. Nestled among Hollywood's labyrinth of glitz and grit, the office was an unexpected epicenter of Amazon's entertainment arm. In this peculiar setting, where fame and fortune were pursued with equal measures of hope and desperation, IMDb became a coveted name. To many in the entertainment industry, an IMDb credit was more than a resume boost—it was a symbol of legitimacy.

We were a small team, but each hire and decision carried the weight of a major feature film as I was part of the interview loop for my manager. Every day, we worked in the shadow of Hollywood's glittering facade, but our mission was different. We weren't after fame but something far more profound: building a team and a culture that could sustain Amazon's long-term growth in the entertainment industry. But amidst the fervor of Hollywood, my mission diverged. While others sought the spotlight, I was building Amazon's footprint in the entertainment industry. My challenge was to bring Amazon's principles into a space that was not only fast paced but also deeply traditional.

Every interview loop I participated into what was a strategic move in Amazon's broader chess game. My approach was grounded in the principle of "Learn and Be Curious," which transformed the way I viewed recruiting. It was about finding people who could evolve, learn, and contribute to the constantly changing environment, not just filling roles. This mindset shaped how we grew the team in Los Angeles and later in London, where we rebuilt an entire office after the previous team had quit.

At Amazon, being curious was about more than just asking questions. It meant challenging the status quo, seeking new knowledge, and always pushing the boundaries of what was possible. My goal was to find people who wanted to dive into ambiguity and come out with new insights. Each hire wasn't just another cog in the machine—it was a carefully chosen piece of the puzzle that could drive the company's next breakthrough. Whether it was engineers, designers, or sales teams, we sought out those who could embrace uncertainty and innovate.

When I joined, mobile was barely a consideration—there were only about 10 million mobile users, and advertisers weren't interested. But within a year, that changed. Mobile exploded, and teams grew exponentially as we rode the wave of innovation in advertising and technology. What seemed like an afterthought became central to Amazon's growth.

The same principle applies to building teams. Hiring wasn't just about solving immediate problems but about scaling for the future. I realized that every hire had a long-term impact. We didn't just need smart people; we needed people who were curious, adaptable, and willing to work through ambiguity. That's why Amazon's leadership principles were so critical. These principles were the foundation for driving growth and innovation across teams worldwide.

One of his famous principles is from Jeff Bezos: "I'd rather interview 50 people and not hire anyone than hire the wrong person." This reflects Amazon's rigorous hiring process, which prioritizes long-term cultural and operational fit over filling a role quickly. This mindset is also reflected in Amazon's culture. In fact, I can attest to actually doing this much interviewing. When I was tasked with helping rebuild Amazon's office in London, I had to interview 40 to 50 people for a single position because we wanted the right person which I will discuss in greater detail later. It was time-consuming and difficult, but finding the right fit meant hiring someone who would stay for years and have a lasting impact. The time invested upfront paid off in the long term, as those individuals helped scale Amazon's presence in the United Kingdom and Europe.

When I look back on my early days at Amazon, it's clear that the company's rapid growth wasn't obvious until we were already in the middle of it. Like many companies, Amazon had its ups and downs. Many people left in the early days, unsure of the company's future. But those who stayed, who embraced curiosity and long-term thinking, witnessed the exponential growth that eventually made Amazon one of the world's largest companies.

Amazon's success wasn't just about luck or timing—it was built on principles that anyone can adopt. By fostering a culture of relentless curiosity and long-term thinking, Amazon was able to scale globally while maintaining its core values. And through that lens, we can see that the greatest opportunities often aren't recognized until you're deep within them. Stay curious, think big, and always be ready to adapt when the moment strikes.

WHAT I LEARNED

1. **BE RELENTLESSLY CURIOUS:** Curiosity is the engine of innovation. Whether building a team or growing personally, always seek new knowledge and improvement. Curiosity drives success and keeps you evolving.

2. **TREAT EVERY DECISION AS CRITICAL:** Every hire, every decision, every shift—it all leaves a mark. Move with purpose, with your eyes wide open, knowing that the choices you make today carve the path your team or company will walk tomorrow. This isn't just business—it's the future you're shaping, whether you realize it or not

3. **BUILD FOR LONG-TERM GROWTH:** Don't focus solely on short-term metrics like revenue. Invest in creating value and fostering a culture of curiosity and innovation. What seems trivial today could become invaluable tomorrow.

CHAPTER 3

LONDON CALLING: NAVIGATING OLD WORLD CHARM WITH NEW AGE PRINCIPLES

"In the middle of difficulty lies opportunity."
— *Albert Einstein*

$\mathcal{I}$n the chaotic rhythm of life, sometimes you've got to ditch the manual and follow your instincts. It's not about overthinking every step but leaping forward with a bias for action because hesitation can mean the difference between triumph and tumble.

Between the relentless rain of Seattle and the sun-soaked ambition of Los Angeles, I carved out a rhythm that kept me grounded in two of America's most dynamic cities. Nearly every other week, I found myself back in Seattle, not just passing through but immersing myself in its pulse. It was here that I met Dan, a visionary leading a groundbreaking initiative that would change everything.

Seattle wasn't just a waypoint; it was where I built genuine connections within every organization I encountered. It wasn't about clocking in or attending meetings—it was about diving deep into conversations, sensing the undercurrents of innovation, and spotting opportunities where others saw none. Dan was a perfect example. Our countless discussions during my frequent trips unveiled mutual passions and aligned goals, creating a synergy that was impossible to ignore.

At a time when the iPhone was still finding its footing and the Amazon shopping app was barely hitting ten million users, mobile advertising was dismissed as a fleeting trend. I remember a senior Sony executive ridiculing the idea, convinced that no one would order anything on such a small screen. But through relentless networking and the invaluable partnership with Dan, I saw the potential others missed. Dan's initiative was exactly the platform I needed to push boundaries and explore uncharted territories.

Our collaboration unlocked a once-in-a-lifetime opportunity: launching a cutting-edge mobile advertising platform across the United Kingdom and Europe. London's Marylebone became my new battleground, a place where history met innovation. Moving there wasn't just a career move; it was a leap into a new cultural landscape, armed with the insights and connections I'd forged in Seattle and Los Angeles.

Living between these two cities, I witnessed constant growth and transformation. Each trip to Seattle reinforced my network, with Dan playing a pivotal role in opening doors I hadn't even considered. Together, we turned skepticism into success, transforming bold ideas into tangible realities across continents.

Ultimately, it wasn't just about expanding a business or launching a product. It was about the people I met, like Dan, the relentless pursuit of innovation, and the unwavering commitment to connecting with those who shared my vision. Through the ebb and flow of Seattle's rain and Los

Angeles'relentless drive, I learned that true growth comes from the relationships you build and the opportunities you seize along the way.

When I first walked into the Amazon London office, it felt like one of those neglected, old-school vinyl stores—where the records had been picked clean, leaving behind echoes of past melodies. The emptiness was palpable, a vacuum left by those who'd moved on, leaving behind a legacy of both pride and challenges. London, with its infamous fog and streets steeped in history, was always a tough nut to crack. Adding a brand that had been in the shadows more than the spotlight only heightened the challenge. Not to mention, this city's high cost of living, even back in 2011, made every decision high stakes.

In the heart of London, as we embarked on the mammoth task of rebuilding the Amazon UK office, we realized this wouldn't be your run-of-the-mill recruitment drive. Our vision was clear and distinct: We weren't looking for the regulars, the nine-to-fivers who walked the well-trodden corporate corridors with rehearsed precision. No, our playbook was different. We sought unconventional, passionate individuals— rebels whose brilliance wasn't crafted in boardrooms but homed in the heartbeats of the city's diverse, pulsating neighborhoods.

Imagine this. An art-school dropout from Camden whose vision is driven by unbridled creativity. A graffiti artist from Shoreditch, painting tales of resilience and ambition. A former educator from Brixton whose lessons stretched beyond classroom walls to global perspectives. Our hiring spree became an expedition to find rare spirits with a spark, those yearning to break free from conventional molds and ready to sculpt new paradigms. Their energy, passion, and unique stories were exactly what we wanted to infuse into our reimagined office.

The urgency to build a high-impact team under tight timelines required creative, guerrilla-style hiring strategies. Traditional recruitment processes were tossed out the window. We dug deep, tapped into our networks, stretched our contacts, and got creative with our outreach. LinkedIn messages, cold calls, impromptu meetings in cafes, and conversations at local pubs became our modus operandi. It was exhilarating and exhausting but necessary to meet our ambitious goals.

Early on, we realized that while expertise and experience had their place, what we truly coveted was adaptability, tenacity, and a hunger to learn. We unearthed diamonds in the rough—individuals who might not fit the "typical" Amazon mold but brought passion and a willingness to evolve. These mavericks, boundary-pushers, became our strongest assets, driving innovation and resilience within the team.

Navigating the cultural landscape of London wasn't without its challenges. Amazon's quintessentially American ethos sometimes clashed with the traditional British work culture. Introducing concepts like Black Friday—a fully American holiday—was met with skepticism. The British, accustomed to their own set of traditions and working styles, found it hard to adopt the high-intensity, customer-obsessed approach that Amazon championed.

Moreover, differing attitudes toward work-life balance posed another hurdle. In the UK, the conventional nine-to-five schedule was the norm, complemented by a pub-driven social culture after work. Amazon's startup-like environment, backed by a publicly traded company's rigor, required longer hours and a different approach to teamwork and collaboration. It was about finding a balance between maintaining local cultural nuances and instilling Amazon's core principles.

As Amazon UK began to experience exponential growth, the pace was breakneck. From a team of twelve, we expanded to over four hundred within three years. This rapid scaling required a strategic approach to hiring—ensuring that each new member not only brought skills but also aligned with Amazon's leadership principles. The hiring process became more rigorous, often involving interviews with forty to fifty candidates for a single position to ensure the right fit. This meticulous approach, though time-consuming, was essential to maintaining the integrity and culture of the team.

Rebuilding Amazon UK was a mosaic of people, experiences, grit, and an unyielding spirit. Amidst London's historic archways and modern skyscrapers, we weren't merely restructuring an office; we were forging an epic of resilience and renaissance. The Amazon ethos became our North Star, guiding us through the whirlwind of change with unwavering anchors: an unrelenting drive to deliver, a deep-seated culture of trust, and the humility to acknowledge when we needed to pivot or learn.

Integrating Amazon's innovative drive with London's traditional charm required a delicate balance of respecting local norms while instilling a relentless pursuit of excellence. The experience underscored the importance of adaptability, creative problem-solving, and hiring for passion and potential rather than just credentials.

In the end, the revival of Amazon UK wasn't just about numbers or Key Performance Indicators (KPIs) but more about people. It was about finding those rare individuals who could embrace Amazon's ethos and contribute to a culture of continuous learning and growth. Amid the historic streets and modern hustle of London, we built something remarkable—an office that stood as a testament to resilience, innovation, and the power of a shared vision.

Amazon's success in the UK mirrored its global trajectory: built on principles that anyone can adopt, fostering a culture of relentless curiosity and long-term thinking. These lessons, learned in the midst of difficulty, highlight that true opportunity often lies within the challenges we face. By embracing action, adaptability, and passion, we not only navigated the complexities of rebuilding an office but also set the foundation for sustained growth and innovation.

WHAT I LEARNED:

1. **Have a Bias for Action**: Move quickly and decisively, especially in high-stakes environments. Hesitation can mean the difference between triumph and tumble.
2. **Be Adaptable**: Embrace unconventional methods when traditional approaches fall short. Flexibility and creativity are key to overcoming unique challenges.
3. **Hire for Passion**: Seek out individuals with hunger and a willingness to learn over conventional qualifications. Passionate employees are more adaptable and committed to the company's long-term vision.

CHAPTER 4

SEATTLE CHRONICLES – GROUND ZERO OF HIRING HUSTLE: THE BAR RAISER

"Character is destiny."
— Heraclitus

*I*n business, it's not just about the journey but the outcomes you produce—the definitive impact you leave behind. Success is measured by the tangible results you deliver after all the hustle and drive.

Relocating to Seattle in 2017 felt like stepping into the eye of a corporate storm. The city, once a haven for grunge aficionados and aficionados of Alice in Chains, The Melvins, and Soundgarden, was morphing under the relentless pressure of Amazon's meteoric rise. The streets that once echoed with the raw riffs of alternative rock were now pulsing with the cadence of ambition and the hum of endless possibilities.

Amazon was at its zenith. Every week, 250 to 500 new souls poured into the city, each one chasing a piece of the Bezos dream. Jeff Bezos himself was still the enigmatic figurehead, orchestrating all-hands meetings with a presence that was both inspiring and unnervingly intense. These gatherings were less about strategy and more about cult-like indoctrination. There was an undercurrent of something almost religious about the way Amazon was being woven into the very fabric of Seattle's identity. It was as if Bezos was not just building a company but a modern-day cathedral of commerce, one that might one day transcend into a belief system should anything happen to its founder.

Living and working in this environment was an exercise in revelation. The closer you got to the "mothership," the more evident Amazon's true nature became. It was a realm where cutthroat competition wasn't just encouraged; it was expected. Colleagues became rivals, and collaboration often gave way to quiet battles for recognition and advancement. The relentless pace and high stakes could wear down even the most resilient spirits, revealing the raw edges of human ambition.

Seattle itself was changing, shedding its identity as the birthplace of grunge and transforming into a symbol of technological prowess. The music that once defined its cultural landscape was being overshadowed by the digital symphony of innovation and enterprise. The city's soul was being redefined, layered with the complexities of growth and the sacrifices that came with it.

Yet, amidst the steel and glass of Amazon's expanding empire, there were lessons to be learned. The city, with all its newfound dynamism, still held pockets of its old self. The lingering echoes of guitar solos and the spirit of rebellion remained, albeit quieter. These remnants served as a reminder that even as Seattle evolved, the essence of its past was not entirely lost.

Relocating to Seattle in 2017 was more than a geographic move; it was an immersion into a microcosm of modern capitalism, where dreams were built at breakneck speed, and the price of success was often personal. It was a place where the shadows of grunge legends lingered, contrasting sharply with the bright lights of corporate ambition. In navigating this landscape, I took away valuable lessons about resilience, the cost of progress, and the ever-changing nature of a city caught between its storied past and an uncertain future.

Seattle, often veiled in moody skies and the misty embrace of Puget Sound, isn't just a city—it's an ecosystem of ambition and competition. I've lived through its evolution, felt its pulse, and seen how Amazon embodies the city's relentless drive. Right in the heart of Seattle, Amazon's sprawling urban campus stands as a testament to this drive, shaped by and shaping the city's identity. It's a city that has grown and thrived on ingenuity, a fusion of old Pacific Northwest roots and cutting-edge tech culture. And Amazon? It's at the epicenter of it all, weaving its relentless pace and customer obsession into the fabric of the city.

Every week, thousands of hopefuls from all corners of the globe aim their aspirations at Amazon, this Seattle-based tech giant. Out of the sea of applications, only 1% made it to the phone screen, and from there, the gauntlet became even more unforgiving. Of the candidates I've seen face-to-face—bright, talented individuals eager to share their stories and prove their worth—less than 10% made it through. Why? Because the ones who succeeded weren't just competent—they unequivocally demonstrated that they had delivered tangible, exceptional results. It wasn't enough to be good; you had to be extraordinary. It was a place where talk was cheap—what mattered was whether you had the receipts to back it up.

Some pivotal roles remained vacant for over a year. Not because there was a lack of applicants but because we were committed to finding the perfect fit. Recall, Jeff Bezos famously said, "I'd rather interview 50 people than hire the wrong one." This philosophy wasn't just corporate rhetoric. It defined the hiring process, ensuring that every new team member wasn't just filling a role but adding to Amazon's evolving narrative. And this was no easy feat—Amazon was expanding rapidly, pushing into new markets and launching innovations at a blistering pace. We needed people who wouldn't just keep up but who would lead the charge.

The Bar Raiser process at Amazon was key to maintaining its culture of excellence, especially during periods of rapid growth. While many companies faced the temptation to lower their hiring standards in times of expansion, Amazon took the opposite approach. The Bar Raiser process was designed to ensure that every hire wasn't just good enough—they had to elevate the team, raise the collective bar, and push the company forward.

At Amazon, a Bar Raiser wasn't just another person in the interview room. They were seasoned interviewers, individuals who were not directly tied to the team hiring, whose sole purpose was to make sure that every new hire was better than at least 50% of the people already in the role. Their independence and expertise ensured that decisions weren't made based on immediate needs or emotional bias but on long-term cultural and performance fit. The focus was on hiring individuals who could not only deliver but also enhance Amazon's DNA, which was built on customer obsession, innovation, and high standards.

In an ideal world, interviews would unfold like a perfectly composed symphony. But in reality, they are often more like an improvisational jazz performance—full of surprises, with no two notes the same. At Amazon, we prided ourselves on a well-orchestrated interview process that minimized the noise of subjectivity and bias. Yet, despite these efforts, there remained a hidden adversary: unconscious bias.

Unconscious bias is the result of the countless experiences, impressions, and stereotypes that shape human judgment. Even the most well-meaning interviewers could fall prey to it. At Amazon, we implemented strategies to combat this, turning to objective behavioral questions that focused on specific business challenges. These questions weren't meant to test personality—they were designed to assess a candidate's ability to handle real-world, complex problems. Coupled with this approach was the STAR technique (Situation, Task, Action, Result), a tool designed to dig deep into candidates' previous experiences. This wasn't small talk—it was more akin to a forensic investigation, with interviewers peeling back layers to get to the core of the candidate's competency.

The result? A rigorous, objective interview process focused less on who a candidate appeared to be and more on what they had accomplished and what they were capable of achieving in the future.

Back in 2017, Seattle was on the brink of transformation. Already a dominant force, Amazon's rapid expansion was reshaping the city's skyline, economy, and cultural identity. By 2019, Seattle had become synonymous with Amazon's relentless growth. What had once been a tech hub was now the global epicenter of innovation, driven largely by the company's insatiable appetite for talent and new ideas. The city's tech scene evolved at lightning speed, and every corner of Seattle seemed to vibrate with the hum of Amazon's impact.

During these pivotal years, Amazon launched several groundbreaking innovations. In 2017, the company introduced Amazon Go, a revolutionary cashier-less shopping experience that removed the friction from the in-store purchasing process. Customers could walk into a store, grab what they needed, and walk out—no checkout lines, no hassle. It was a glimpse into the future of retail, made possible by Amazon's deep investment in technology.

But Amazon Go was just the beginning. That same year, the company released the Amazon Echo Show, a device that combined the power of Alexa with a screen, transforming the way consumers interacted with smart home devices. AWS continued to dominate the cloud computing market, rolling out products like SageMaker, which made building AI models accessible to companies without needing deep expertise. These were not mere product launches—they were statements of intent, signaling Amazon's commitment to redefine not just retail but the way the world operated.

Seattle itself became a reflection of this relentless pace. The skyline was dominated by Amazon's expanding urban campus, with new towers rising almost as quickly as teams could fill them. Neighborhoods like South Lake Union transformed from sleepy districts into bustling hubs of tech activity. Cafes and coworking spaces buzzed with the conversations of Amazon employees, and the city's population swelled as new hires poured in. Housing prices skyrocketed, and infrastructure struggled to keep up, but the energy of growth was undeniable.

But for all the rapid growth, there was a challenge unique to Seattle: the Seattle Freeze. This term, coined to describe the city's infamous social aloofness, was more than just a social quirk—it was a barrier. In Seattle, casual politeness didn't often translate into deep connections. Conversations rarely led to lasting relationships, and many newcomers found it difficult to break into the tightly knit social circles that had formed over the years.

For businesses, the Seattle Freeze presented a different kind of challenge. Breaking into the city's tech scene, forming partnerships, and building teams required persistence. Seattleites, while friendly on the surface, took time to warm up to new people and ideas. It was easy to mistake the polite distance for reluctance or disinterest, but the truth was more nuanced. Seattle was a city where relationships, especially in business, were built slowly over time.

Amazon's expansion from 2017 to 2019 wasn't just about filling seats—it was about creating a scalable ecosystem that could handle the pressures of a global company. Every action during this period became part of a broader narrative, one that was being written in real-time. The lesson here is clear: growth isn't just about moving fast—it's about leaving an indelible mark, producing real outcomes, and navigating expansion with intention and excellence.

In the end, success is measured not by how quickly you grow but by the lasting impact you create. At Amazon, every new hire, every product launch, and every business decision was driven by a relentless focus on outcomes. And that, ultimately, is what sets Amazon apart—it's not just about the journey; it's about what you leave behind.

WHAT I LEARNED:

1. **Consistency Builds Trust**: In Seattle, consistency is key to building trust. Just as relationships take time to form, businesses need to show up consistently to earn trust. Delivering on promises, maintaining your values, and following through on commitments gradually break down barriers.

2. **Patience is Key**: Building meaningful relationships, whether in business or personal life, requires patience. In Seattle, this is especially true. Rushing to close deals or form connections won't yield long-term results. Take the time to understand your partners, clients, and employees, and allow trust to develop organically.

3. **Authentic Engagement**: The Seattle Freeze isn't about ignoring people—it's about a preference for deeper, more meaningful connections. In business, this translates to a focus on authentic engagement. Shallow interactions won't break the ice, but genuine interest in people's stories, needs, and challenges will.

4. **Play the Long Game**: Building trust and loyalty, whether with employees or clients, is a long-term investment. The best relationships take time to cultivate, but the rewards of patience and consistency are long-lasting. In fast-growing environments, playing the long game is crucial to building strong, enduring connections.

5. **Maintain Rigorous Standards**: Even during periods of rapid growth, don't compromise on hiring the right people. The quality of your team directly impacts the quality of

your product, service, and customer experience. Every hire should raise the bar and push the company forward.

6. **Adapt but Keep Core Values Intact**: While Amazon's expansion transformed Seattle, the company stayed grounded in its core values. Customer obsession, innovation, and a commitment to operational excellence were non-negotiable. These values served as a guiding light during periods of rapid change.

7. **Invest in Infrastructure**: As your company grows, so do the external factors—housing, transportation, logistics—that support your employees. Amazon's growth didn't just add new buildings to Seattle's skyline; it reshaped the city's infrastructure. For any company experiencing rapid expansion, ensuring that both internal systems and external partnerships can handle the pressures of growth is critical.

CHAPTER 5

THE STAR METHOD – STRIPPING AWAY THE FLUFF TO GET TO THE CORE

> *"Man is nothing else but what he makes of himself."*
> — Jean-Paul Sartre

*I*t's a wild world out there, full of people spinning grand tales of their achievements and promising future success. But if life has taught us anything, it's that your past is often the best predictor of your future. As a Bar Raiser at Amazon, I wasn't looking for smooth narrators who could string together impressive words—I was hunting for doers. The questions we asked were designed to dig deep, to unearth the unvarnished stories of real challenges, struggles, and triumphs. I wasn't interested in tall tales or exaggerated accomplishments. I wanted the gritty truth, the raw narrative of how someone confronted adversity and came out the other side.

In the world of work, as in life, there are no shortcuts, no rehearsed answers that will carry you through. Like an underground rock song, life's toughest moments come at us unexpectedly and unfiltered. That's what I was looking for in an Amazon candidate: not the ones who only had tales of victories, but the ones who had been through the trenches,

27

faced uncertainty, gotten bruised, and emerged wiser, ready to tell a tale worth hearing. The STAR Method was our tool of choice to filter out the fluff and get to the core of who a candidate really was.

Imagine sitting across from someone eager to land their dream job at Amazon. They come in polished, confident, and prepared to answer questions. But what separates those who make it from those who don't isn't just their resume or the brand names they've worked with—it's how they respond when the room heats up, when the questions demand more than surface-level answers.

As a Bar Raiser, I had one job: to ensure that the people we brought on board were exceptional, not just good. And to do that, I needed to cut through the stories, the rehearsed anecdotes, and the flashy resumes. The STAR Method allowed me to do that. It gave me a lens through which I could see the truth behind every narrative.

When someone started telling me about a time they achieved a significant goal or overcame a challenge, I wasn't just listening for the end result. I wanted to hear how they got there. What did they do when the plan fell apart? How did they navigate the chaos? What decisions did they make when everything was on the line? The STAR Method helped me get past the superficial and dig into the decisions, actions, and results that defined who they were.

Sample Question:

"Tell me about a time when you had significant, unanticipated obstacles to overcome in achieving a key goal. What was the obstacle? Were you eventually successful? Knowing what you know now, is there anything you would have done differently?"

What I'm really saying with this question is: Take me back. Show me a moment where the odds weren't in your favor, where life threw you a curveball, and you were gunning for success but hit a wall. Tell me about that wall. Did you scale it, or did it knock you down? And more importantly, in those quiet moments of reflection, what would you change about how you handled that situation? What regrets or lessons are etched into your professional journey today?

It's not about perfection—it never was. It's about how you grew, how you evolved, and how you faced the storm. What I want to see is not just your ability to win but your ability to reflect and learn. Those who succeed at Amazon aren't just the victors; they're the self-critical, those who understand the why behind every decision they made. Did you pull off the unthinkable, or did you fall short and rise again? That's the essence of the STAR method—it's not about scripted answers; it's about digging into the truth of your experience.

So, you've asked a behavioral question. Now it's time to apply the STAR method to reel in the real story: Situation, Task, Action, Result. This method strips away the glitz and fluff, forcing candidates to focus on what really matters—their ability to solve problems and deliver results. The one part of the "classic" STAR method that I would rephrase would be the first part – Story and Tension. Story and tension are the heartbeat of the STAR method. It's not just about rattling off facts—it's about pulling people into a moment, making them feel the pressure, the stakes, the grit of the situation. Without tension, it's just a checklist. But when you bring in the struggle and the payoff, that's where the story comes alive. That's where they see who you really are.

Here's how it works:

Story

Set the stage. Every good story has a backdrop. We need to understand the context—the environment, the pressures, the urgency. What was the challenge? What was at stake? Who was involved? Were the odds stacked against them?

Tension

If there's no tension, there's no story. Tension is what makes the STAR method more than just a dry script. It's the pulse in the story—the challenge that put you on the edge, the stakes that made it real. Without tension, it's just another task you checked off. But when you lay out the pressure, the obstacles, and how you pushed through, that's when people lean in. That's when they see what you're really made of.

Action

This is the heart of the story. What did they *do*? We're not looking for passive bystanders; we want the main character, the one who rolled up their sleeves and took action. How did they handle the situation? What strategies did they use? How did they navigate the obstacles in their way?

Result

The climax—what happened as a result of their actions? Did they succeed or fail? What was the outcome? This is where the story gets real. Success isn't the only metric—sometimes failure teaches the most profound lessons. Did they grow? Did they learn something that changed how they approach challenges in the future?

The most valuable stories come from real experiences, not hypotheticals. That's why the STAR method is so effective— it forces candidates to talk about specific, lived moments where they faced challenges and had to make decisions under pressure. Here's an example of how a STAR-based interview might play out:

Story:

"We were launching a new product that was a first of its kind that was going to disrupt the market, and three days before the deadline, when our main supplier went under.

Tension:

"Without this component, the entire project would be delayed, which would disrupt all of our cash flow.

Action:

"I immediately called an emergency meeting with the design and procurement teams. We brainstormed alternatives, identified a new supplier within 24 hours, and modified the design to accommodate the changes. I worked through the night to renegotiate contracts and streamline the supply chain to meet our deadline."

Result:

"We launched on time, despite the setback, and the product went on to exceed sales projections by 20% in its first quarter."

This is the kind of story that resonates. It's real, it's specific, and it shows not just success but problem-solving under pressure. The STAR method doesn't allow for generalizations or fluff—it forces candidates to talk about what really matters.

Sometimes, the story you get isn't enough. Maybe the candidate glosses over key details or focuses too much on the outcome without explaining how they got there. When that happens, it's your job as an interviewer to dig deeper. Here are some questions you can use to get more out of their story:

Why this situation? Why did this particular challenge stand out among others? What made it significant?

How overwhelming was the obstacle? Did they feel like they were staring down an impossible task? How did they assess the magnitude of the challenge?

What might have happened if they didn't act? What was the risk of failure, and how did that impact their decision-making process?

These questions pull back the curtain, showing how the candidate thinks under pressure and how they make decisions in moments that matter.

The STAR method isn't just a tool for uncovering stories—it's a method for understanding how people think, act, and deliver. When used correctly, it helps you understand not just what someone has done, but how they approach challenges and what drives their decision-making process.

In the grand tapestry of Amazon's hiring process, the details of a single interview might seem like mere threads. But those threads are critical—each one could mean the difference between hiring someone who raises the bar or someone who fades into the background. When we sat in debriefs, the focus was singular: Did this candidate deliver? And how did they do it?

In those debriefs, there was no room for vagueness or ambiguity. We wanted proof—concrete examples of success, clear results that demonstrated the candidate's ability to make an impact. Sometimes, we found ourselves on the edge of our seats, dissecting a candidate's every word, searching for that key fact or action that could tip the scales in their favor.

Being a Bar Raiser was about more than just hiring someone to fill a position. It was about shaping Amazon's future, ensuring that each new hire wasn't just qualified but capable of propelling the company forward. In the intense environment of those debriefs, every opinion mattered, but in the end, the Bar Raiser had the final say, guarding the integrity of Amazon's hiring standards.

While the STAR method is powerful, there are pitfalls to avoid in an interview:

Avoid hypotheticals. Asking what someone would do in a hypothetical situation is easy to game. You want to know what they did, not what they would do.

Don't be swayed by shiny resumes. Just because someone worked at a big-name company or attended an Ivy League school doesn't mean they can deliver. The STAR method helps you get past the resume glitter and focus on real achievements.

Don't get caught in riddles. There's no value in throwing curveball riddles or abstract puzzles at candidates. They're not going to help you find out whether someone can solve real-world problems. Stick to behavioral questions that reveal concrete actions and results.

When you're interviewing someone, typing away on a laptop can create a wall between you and the person across from you. Sure, it feels efficient, but it kills the vibe. Instead, walk into the room with your questions already thought out— write them down or mentally prepare in advance. Think of it like a great conversation. When you're truly engaged, you won't need to go back to your notes to remember the key details—it will stick with you.

It's like hearing *Welcome to the Jungle* by Guns N' Roses for the first time—you don't need to scribble down the lyrics. "You know where you are? You're in the jungle, baby!" sticks with you because it hits hard, right out of the gate. Or take an iconic moment from *Game of Thrones*: "When you play the game of thrones, you win or you die." You don't forget it because it's not just words—it's a gut punch. The best interviews work the same way. When someone says something that matters, you'll remember. Look them in the eye, really listen. Let the conversation flow naturally, and you'll walk away with more than just notes—you'll have a real connection. The most powerful moments aren't transcribed—they're felt.

At the end of the day, the STAR method isn't about telling good stories—it's about delivering results. We weren't interested in candidates who only talked about potential. We wanted people who could point to specific moments where they made a real difference. And the STAR method allowed us to find those people.

One of my favorite books is **"20 Master Plots"** by Ronald Tobias shows that every great story follows a classic structure—whether it's a quest, revenge, or transformation. The same goes for the **STAR method** in interviews. It's not just facts; it's **Story** and **Tension**.

Your *Situation* sets the scene, the *Task* builds the stakes, the *Action* shows how you handled the heat, and the *Result* delivers the payoff. Without tension, it's just noise. With it, you're the protagonist they won't forget.

WHAT I LEARNED:

1. **Deliver Tangible Results**: Focus on outcomes and measurable impact. In business, potential isn't enough—you need to prove that you can deliver, especially under pressure. This is what sets top candidates apart from the rest.

2. **Hire High Standards**: Pursue exceptional candidates, even if it means the hiring process takes longer or the role stays unfilled for a while. The short-term cost is worth the long-term benefit of bringing in someone who can truly elevate the team. As a Bar Raiser, I've driven people crazy by insisting we continue the search for the right person, sometimes conducting 50 interviews for a single role. It was expensive, yes, but settling for mediocrity costs far more in the long run.

3. **Embrace Continuous Learning**: The STAR method isn't just about success—it's about learning from both wins and losses. Behavioral interviews dissect those critical moments to extract lessons that fuel future growth and innovation. Every candidate has a journey, and the ones who've learned the most along the way are often the ones who will propel your company forward.

CHAPTER 6

SYDNEY'S SIRENS – HIRING DOWN UNDER AND OVERCOMING THE WAVES

"The strength of the team is each individual member. The strength of each member is the team."
— *Phil Jackson*

*I*n the hodgepodge of life's bustling bazaar, trust is the currency that circulates with a hushed nod, a whispered promise, and a shared journey through uncharted lanes. It's a pact forged not by signed papers but by the unspoken understanding that we're all wanderers on the same convoluted path, searching for kindred souls to light the way.

Australia, with its vast and untamed landscapes, deep cultural roots, and a fierce sense of independence, doesn't easily bow to newcomers. There's an innate resilience, a spirit that stands tall in the face of foreign influence, especially from global giants. When Amazon cast its gaze toward the Land Down Under, it wasn't the physical distance that was the challenge. It was bridging the cultural chasm, the unspoken skepticism that greeted this corporate titan.

Australia wasn't in awe of Amazon's global stature; instead, it met the e-commerce juggernaut with a wary glance. The media had already amplified the image of Amazon as a corporate behemoth ready to colonize local markets, squash small businesses, and force-feed an American ethos onto Australian soil. Amazon wasn't just another company—it became a symbol of perceived American overreach.

The sentiment was palpable: Amazon was seen as an outsider, a force that wasn't going to enhance but erode what Australians held dear. The brand carried the weight of all the presumptions Australians had about America—audacious, overwhelming, and always on the move. And when Amazon finally set foot on Australian soil, the suspicion was clear: this wasn't just a business move; it was a cultural confrontation.

For Amazon, the challenge wasn't simply about launching in a new market; it was about recalibrating its approach. Setting up logistics, launching the marketplace—these were logistical hurdles. But the real task was subtler, more profound. It was about building trust in a land that deeply values authenticity, community, and local pride.

The initial recruitment phase felt less like hiring and more like a delicate cultural dance. Every interview was an attempt to decode the Australian psyche, to dismantle biases and to extend a hand of mutual respect. The question wasn't just whether someone was right for Amazon, but whether Amazon could be right for Australia.

To do this, we had to confront the narrative that we were yet another American company storming in with grand ambitions but little regard for the local pulse. And we had to do it one conversation at a time.

Instead of flashy presentations or lofty promises, we chose to connect through stories. Not Amazon's success stories, but human stories—of employees from around the world.

In every interview and conversation, we shared tales of the people behind the corporate façade: the coder who was also a novelist, the manager who spent weekends teaching dance to underprivileged kids, or the executive who religiously logged off in the evening to read bedtime stories to her daughter across the globe.

These stories weren't just PR gimmicks—they were the bridge between Amazon and the local community. We wanted to show that Amazon was more than just a monolithic entity and that behind the brand were people, each with their own passions, struggles, and aspirations. This approach resonated with Australians, who value authenticity and personal connection over corporate gloss.

We didn't stop there. We embedded ourselves in the community, not in boardrooms but in local parks, pubs, and over rugby matches. These informal settings became key to forging real connections. The Aussies didn't want corporate sales pitches; they wanted genuine conversations. Slowly, Amazon began to shed its image of a foreign invader and started being viewed as a brand that could contribute positively to their culture.

Despite our initial efforts, we made our fair share of mistakes. We underestimated how much trust needed to be earned in Australia. We launched with a vision that felt too American, too loud. In those early days, Amazon wasn't embraced. The resistance wasn't just business skepticism. It was also cultural.

One of the key lessons we learned was that Australians weren't going to be wowed by Amazon's global reputation. The brand's size, power, and technological prowess weren't selling points here. They valued local connections, small businesses, and community spirit. So, we pivoted.

We began working closely with local manufacturers to create private labels that resonated with the Australian ethos. Take Cuddly Bubs, a brand of nappies made locally in Australia, designed specifically to meet local needs and preferences. The phrase "Cuddly Bubs" itself is inherently Aussie, a colloquialism that immediately felt authentic.

We also launched Amazon's first innovation grant program in Australia, providing financial support to small businesses across the country. This wasn't just about providing grants; it was about showing that Amazon wasn't here to dominate but to help local businesses thrive. These grants were a direct response to the concerns we had heard—concerns that Amazon would just copy their products, undercut prices, and then ship them overseas. Instead, we were investing in their success, helping them grow and reach new customers.

One particularly poignant example was WAW Handplanes, a business that made hand planes out of recycled plastic from the Great Barrier Reef. This brand not only captured the eco-conscious ethos of Australia but also gave back to the environment by planting trees for every purchase made. Partnering with businesses like WAW Handplanes allowed Amazon to tap into the values that Australians hold dear—sustainability, nature, and community responsibility.

It wasn't an overnight transformation. Australians are deeply proud of their culture, and they weren't going to embrace Amazon until we proved that we respected their values. It took time—time spent on listening tours, time spent in the community, and time spent showing through actions, not words, that Amazon was here to stay and to contribute.

Eventually, Amazon was no longer seen as an outsider. By embedding ourselves in the culture, we started to build relationships that transcended business. Our employees weren't just workers—they became ambassadors for the brand, helping to share our values and build trust in their communities. It was through this grassroots approach that we began to change perceptions.

Fast-forward to the present, and Amazon Australia is no longer viewed with suspicion. The company has found its rhythm here, not by force but through respect. The team we built is a patchwork of diverse talent, each bringing something unique to the table and each helping to tell the Amazon story in a way that resonates with local values.

Whether it was learning the significance of an Aussie sport or understanding the pride Australians take in their heritage, Amazon Australia became a partner, not a disruptor. And that partnership has paid dividends—Amazon Australia is now a respected player in the local market, known for both its global reach and its commitment to supporting local businesses.

WHAT I LEARNED:

1. **Invest in Local Understanding**: Before entering any new market, invest in deeply understanding local values, traditions, and expectations. Listening isn't just an exercise; it's essential for earning trust.

2. **Humanize Your Brand**: Move beyond the corporate veneer and share real stories about your people—their passions, struggles, and achievements. This builds a connection that resonates far more than any polished presentation ever could.

3. **Earn Trust Through Humility**: Don't be afraid to admit your mistakes and be transparent about your challenges. Humility and authenticity will always resonate more than a polished success story.

4. **Embed Into the Community**: To build trust, businesses need to meet people where they are—not just in boardrooms, but in parks, at sporting events, and over casual conversations. Make the effort to integrate, not dominate.

CHAPTER 7

BAR RAISER RITES – THE ELITE GUARD OF AMAZON'S INTERVIEWING GAUNTLET

"The function of education is to teach one to think intensively and to think critically."
— Martin Luther King Jr.

*E*mbracing the Bar Raiser program infuses hiring with a symphony of impartiality and potential discovery, ensuring that each hire resonates with enduring excellence. Whether you're a seasoned corporation or a budding startup, adopting this ethos enriches your journey by uncovering hidden brilliance and fostering a culture of exceptional hires.

Hiring is a craft, an intricate dance choreographed with purpose and intent. Think of the process as more than just filling a position or ticking off boxes on a checklist. It's a deeply involved ritual, and at Amazon, it's taken to an art form that is part of its core operating principles—the famed Bar Raiser program. It's not just about making sure someone can do the job; it's about ensuring that they elevate the entire team, raising the standard for everyone around them.

Amazon's 14 Leadership Principles act as both a guide and a filter in the hiring process. They aren't just words painted on office walls; they are an intrinsic part of Amazon's DNA. Every step in the hiring process, from the very first phone screen to the final decision in the debrief, is measured against these principles. Candidates aren't just asked if they can code or sell or manage—they are tested on how they think, how they make decisions, how they work under pressure, and how they innovate for the customer.

For those of us conducting interviews, these principles are more than guidelines. They are the foundation on which Amazon's hiring decisions rest, ensuring that new hires don't just fill gaps but actively push the organization forward.

Bar Raisers are a select group at Amazon, charged with a singular mission: to ensure that every hire raises the bar. The term itself might sound curious to outsiders, but its origin is rooted in a mission of continuous improvement. It's a philosophy built into Amazon's hiring system since 1999, when the 'barkeeper program' evolved into the Bar Raiser program. These individuals are gatekeepers of Amazon's talent pipeline, tasked with ensuring that no candidate is hired unless they demonstrate a clear ability to raise the performance level of their team.

A Bar Raiser is not just another interviewer. They don't come from the team making the hire, which gives them a uniquely objective viewpoint. Their role isn't to assess a candidate's technical skills—that's the responsibility of the hiring manager and the functional interviewers. The Bar Raiser's job is to ensure that the candidate will be a long-term cultural fit, align with Amazon's Leadership Principles, and most importantly, that they will elevate the company's standards.

The Bar Raiser program isn't just about protecting Amazon's hiring standards. It's about driving growth, innovation, and customer obsession. By ensuring that each new hire brings something exceptional to the table, Amazon maintains a high level of internal competition, which keeps the company agile and forward-thinking. And while Bar Raisers act as objective third parties in the interview process, they are also mentors—guiding hiring managers, providing feedback, and helping to ensure that the process isn't just about filling an empty seat but about shaping the future of the company.

Being a Bar Raiser isn't a title that's given lightly. It's a role earned through experience, deep knowledge of the company's Leadership Principles, and the ability to objectively assess talent. Bar Raisers undergo specialized training to ensure that they can effectively guide the hiring process. They are often high performers within their teams, but their role as a Bar Raiser takes precedence when they step into the hiring realm.

Their responsibilities include:

Maintaining Objectivity: Because Bar Raisers come from outside the hiring team, they provide an impartial perspective. This prevents the hiring manager from being biased toward a candidate simply because they're in a rush to fill the role.

Evaluating Potential: Bar Raisers aren't looking for someone who can just do the job today. They're looking for someone who can grow, adapt, and continue to excel in the future.

Ensuring Cultural Fit: Bar Raisers are the guardians of Amazon's culture. They make sure every candidate fits into the broader company vision and aligns with Amazon's Leadership Principles.

Consulting with the Hiring Team: After the interviews, Bar Raisers act as consultants, providing feedback and guiding hiring managers in making the final decision.

The Bar Raiser doesn't just check off boxes; they are the keystone of Amazon's interview process. Without their approval, no hire is made.

The Bar Raiser philosophy ensures that every new hire is a step forward. There's no settling for "good enough." Candidates must exceed expectations, bringing something new to the table that will push their team to new heights. This approach fosters a culture of high performance, where every hire is expected to make a measurable impact.

Think about the ripple effect this has on the company's culture. Each new hire raises the bar, which in turn raises the expectations for everyone else. It's a self-sustaining cycle of continuous improvement.

At Amazon, the concept of raising the bar goes beyond the Bar Raiser program. Every employee, regardless of their role, is expected to raise the bar. It's a core part of the company's culture. This means that if you want to be promoted, you must already be performing at the next level. It's not enough to do your job well; you need to be doing the job above yours, without the title or the pay, before you can be considered for a promotion.

Take the example of Sarah, a mid-level manager in AWS. She had been excelling in her role for five years—managing her team, bringing in new clients, and refining processes. But when she applied for a senior leadership position, the feedback was clear: "You're not operating at the next level yet." In other words, she wasn't already doing the work of the role she was aiming for. Over the next few months, Sarah took on additional responsibilities, leading initiatives that weren't officially hers and pushing herself beyond her comfort zone.

She wasn't just doing her job anymore; she was operating at the level above her. Only then, after months of proving herself, did she earn the promotion.

This is the essence of raising the bar at Amazon. You don't get the title and then rise to the occasion; you rise to the occasion first, and only then are you given the title.

In the world of the Bar Raiser, every hire is a critical decision. It's not about filling a position for today; it's about ensuring that the person you bring in will elevate the team for years to come. The Bar Raiser ensures that the hiring process isn't just about finding someone who can do the job—it's about finding someone who will redefine the job.

Bar Raisers ask the tough questions. They aren't just looking for competence—they're looking for candidates who will push their team to new heights. They challenge candidates with behavioral questions designed to uncover how they've handled adversity, how they've raised the bar in previous roles, and how they align with Amazon's Leadership Principles.

While the Bar Raiser program is synonymous with Amazon, its principles can be applied to any organization. Whether you're a startup looking to build your team from scratch or an established company seeking to improve your hiring process, the Bar Raiser ethos can help you make better hiring decisions.

WHAT I LEARNED:

1. **Start Small**: You don't need to have a large number of Bar Raisers to start. Begin with a few trusted employees who deeply understand your company's culture and values. These individuals will act as the gatekeepers for hiring decisions, ensuring that every new hire raises the bar.

2. **Maintain Objectivity**: Bar Raisers should not be directly involved with the team making the hire. This creates a layer of impartiality that helps prevent biases and ensures that candidates are evaluated based on their potential and fit with the company's culture.

3. **Offer Continuous Training**: Keep your Bar Raisers up to date on the latest hiring trends and best practices. Provide them with ongoing support and feedback to help them refine their skills.

4. **Celebrate Successes**: When your Bar Raisers make great hires, celebrate those successes. Recognizing their efforts helps keep them engaged and motivated to continue raising the bar for your organization.

5. **Incentivize Excellence**: Reward Bar Raisers for their contributions, whether through bonuses, promotions, or public recognition. Acknowledging their efforts will reinforce the importance of the program and motivate others to participate.

CHAPTER 8

THE LEADERSHIP PRINCIPLE TIGHTROPE – BALANCING CULTURE AND INDIVIDUALITY

"It is not the strongest of the species that survive, nor the most intelligent, but the one most responsive to change."
— *Charles Darwin*

avigating the tumultuous seas of leadership, having a set of principles is like having a compass in a storm. It's the beacon that guides you through the chaos, reminding you that in the cacophony of culture and individuality, the keynotes of trust, results, and customer focus are what compose the symphony of success.

Leadership, in its essence, is about finding balance. For startups and established organizations alike, there's a fine line between cultivating a strong, cohesive company culture and allowing individual creativity to flourish. This tightrope walk is critical, especially in environments like Amazon, where innovation thrives but must always be aligned with a set of deeply ingrained principles. Leadership at Amazon isn't about rigid conformity, but it also isn't about unchecked individualism. It's about striking the right chord between these two forces.

Amazon's Leadership Principles serve as the foundation for how decisions are made, how teams operate, and how success is measured. These principles aren't just guidelines—they're deeply embedded into the very fabric of the company. They act as a decision-making framework that governs everything from hiring to product development to customer interactions.

Yet, these principles don't stifle individuality or creativity. Instead, they create an environment where creative thinking is structured and directed toward meaningful outcomes. They provide the guardrails that keep the company moving in the right direction while allowing individuals to push boundaries and explore new frontiers.

At the heart of Amazon's Leadership Principles is Customer Obsession. For Amazon, the customer isn't just important—they are everything. Every product, every service, every decision is viewed through the lens of how it benefits the customer. It's a philosophy that drives the company to innovate relentlessly.

But customer obsession isn't just about satisfying immediate needs. It's about anticipating what customers will want in the future, often before they even realize it themselves. Amazon's ability to continuously innovate and disrupt industries stems from its commitment to working backward from the customer's needs.

For startups, this principle is equally powerful. Too often, founders fall in love with their technology or product without considering whether it truly solves a customer problem. Steve Jobs once said, "Customers don't know what they want until we've shown them." Yet, he was also adamant that the product must seamlessly integrate into the customer's life. It's about making things easy, intuitive, and meaningful. Amazon applies this rigorously, always asking: "How does this solve a customer problem?"

Consider Amazon's Just Walk Out technology, launched in 2017. The idea was simple: Eliminate the checkout line by letting customers scan their phones, grab what they needed, and leave the store. It was innovative, solving a real problem—customers wasting time in long lines during their lunch break. But fast forward to 2024, and the context has changed.

Having lived in Nashville for a bit, I walked past Amazon's *Just Walk Out* store more times than I can count at BNA airport. And every time, it was the same story—an empty space, an eerie silence, an employee waiting to explain to someone how to come in as they scroll aimlessly on their phone because nobody is coming inside, and a million-dollar piece of technology collecting metaphorical dust.

The promise was simple: frictionless, cashier-free shopping. A marvel of AI and automation, designed to revolutionize retail. But here's the problem—when foot traffic is low, margins are razor-thin, and the cost to implement the technology is sky-high, the math just doesn't work.

The pandemic didn't just shift how we work—it redefined where we exist. Office buildings never fully repopulated, public spaces remain underutilized, and the necessity for tech like *Just Walk Out* has evaporated. Take Hudson Nonstop at the airport—once marketed as a futuristic convenience, now a clunky, over-engineered solution to a problem that no longer exists. A space that's rarely busy enough to justify the cost, a perfect example of innovation that made sense in a pre-pandemic world but feels completely disconnected from reality now.

This is the hard truth of technology: just because you can build it, doesn't mean people will use it. When the world shifts, businesses have to pivot—otherwise, you're left with an expensive, empty store that no one actually needs.

Amazon's leadership recognized this shift and pivoted, reallocating resources where they could provide greater value. This adaptability, guided by the principle of customer obsession, allowed Amazon to continuously evolve.

Innovation is only meaningful if it leads to results. At Amazon, Deliver Results is another cornerstone principle, ensuring that great ideas are always tied to measurable outcomes. Leaders aren't just idea generators; they are responsible for ensuring those ideas come to fruition and provide real value to the business.

In a high-growth environment, it's easy to get caught up in grand visions and lose sight of the need to deliver tangible outcomes. Leaders at Amazon are tasked with not only setting ambitious goals but also making sure they are achieved. This focus on results ensures that innovation doesn't happen in a vacuum—it drives the company forward.

Startups, in particular, can benefit from this principle. While the early days of building a company may be fueled by creativity and experimentation, long-term success requires discipline. It's not enough to have a great idea; you must execute that idea, measure its success, and iterate based on results.

A critical aspect of delivering results is making hard decisions. Leaders must often navigate difficult trade-offs, prioritizing what will move the needle for the business and de-prioritizing or cutting projects that aren't performing. At Amazon, this focus on accountability creates a culture where leaders are expected to own their decisions fully—both the successes and the failures.

The principle of Earn Trust is another vital thread in Amazon's leadership philosophy. Trust is the currency that makes everything else possible—it allows teams to take risks, experiment, and innovate without fear of retribution. At Amazon, leaders are expected to build trust both within their teams and with external partners, creating an environment where open, honest communication can flourish.

Earning trust isn't just about being reliable or competent; it's about fostering an environment where dissenting opinions are welcomed and encouraged. Leaders who earn trust are those who can listen to others, admit when they're wrong, and create space for diverse perspectives. They empower their teams to speak up, challenge assumptions, and contribute to the company's broader mission.

Startups, in particular, must build trust quickly. Without the track record or brand recognition of larger organizations, trust becomes even more critical. Founders and leaders who can establish a culture of trust early on will find it easier to attract top talent, secure investment, and build lasting relationships with customers and partners.

Leadership at Amazon involves walking a tightrope between enforcing a strong, cohesive culture and allowing for individual creativity and innovation. This balance is critical to maintaining a culture of high performance without stifling the unique contributions of each team member.

Startups often face the same challenge. In the early stages of building a company, culture is malleable. It's shaped by the founders' vision and the initial team members who join the company. But as the company grows, maintaining that culture while encouraging individuality becomes more difficult. Too much emphasis on culture can stifle innovation, while too much focus on individuality can create fragmentation and misalignment.

At Amazon, this balance is achieved by aligning every team member's work with the Leadership Principles. These principles act as a guiding framework, allowing individuals to express their creativity and drive innovation while ensuring that their efforts are aligned with the company's broader mission.

The beauty of Amazon's Leadership Principles is their interconnectedness. Customer obsession drives innovation, which in turn leads to the ability to deliver results. As leaders consistently deliver results, they earn trust within the organization and with external stakeholders. And as trust grows, so does the ability to take on bigger, bolder challenges. It's a virtuous cycle that drives long-term success.

For startups and established companies alike, these principles provide a roadmap for creating a culture of continuous improvement. They offer a framework for balancing the need for a strong, cohesive culture with the need to foster individuality and innovation. By embracing these principles, leaders can build organizations that are agile, resilient, and primed for success.

WHAT I LEARNED:

1. **Start with the Customer**: Whether you're building a product, developing a service, or entering a new market, always start by asking, "How does this solve a customer problem?" If you can't answer that question, it's time to go back to the drawing board.

2. **Deliver Tangible Results**: Ideas are only as good as their execution. Focus on delivering outcomes that can be measured, and make sure your team is accountable for achieving those outcomes.

3. **Earn Trust Early**: Building trust is essential for startups, where relationships with investors, partners, and early customers can make or break the business. Create an environment where trust can flourish by fostering open communication and empowering your team to challenge assumptions.

4. **Balance Culture and Individuality**: As your startup grows, make sure you maintain a strong culture while encouraging individual creativity and innovation. Use guiding principles to align your team's efforts with the company's broader mission, ensuring that innovation is directed toward meaningful outcomes.

CHAPTER 9

ROOKIES, VETS, AND THE IN-BETWEENS – TALES OF INTERVIEWING

"Excellence is never an accident. It is the result of high intention, sincere effort, and intelligent execution."
— Aristotle

*I*n the grand bazaar of corporate giants, Amazon stands as a colossal marketplace of innovation and ambition. Within its sprawling corridors and endless meeting rooms lies a complex tapestry of individuals—the rookies, the vets, and those suspended somewhere in between. Each group weaves its own thread into the corporate fabric, shaping and reshaping the culture in ways both overt and subtle. And though the walls echo with talk of disruptive technology and groundbreaking ideas, the game remains the same: it's not just what you know but who you know.

This chapter dives deep into the world of interviews, showcasing how different types of candidates—rookies, veterans, and those in between—navigate Amazon's intricate hiring process. It also unveils the unspoken truth about corporate culture: it's often as much about social dynamics and relationships as it is about performance. Interviews are not merely a test of your qualifications but an assessment of how well you will fit within this ever-evolving ecosystem.

Rookies at Amazon arrive with wide eyes and hearts full of ambition. They are bright-eyed adventurers stepping into a world that promises endless possibilities and challenges. Their résumés might boast Ivy League educations or groundbreaking projects, but as they navigate the interview process, they quickly realize it's not just about showcasing their technical skills or innovative ideas. Here, it's about storytelling—crafting a narrative that aligns their personal journey with Amazon's legendary Leadership Principles.

The interview process for rookies at Amazon can feel like a crucible. Behavioral questions probe not just for past achievements but for evidence of Amazon's hallowed tenets: customer obsession, ownership, and bias for action. Rookies must translate their fledgling experiences into tales of resilience, creativity, and impact. The STAR method—Situation, Task, Action, Result—is the framework by which they tell their stories. And make no mistake: it's an art, not a science. Those who master it find themselves welcomed into the fold, while those who falter quickly learn that Amazon's standards for success are exacting.

Yet, even after landing the job, the challenges are far from over. Rookies must quickly learn the unspoken rules of the game. KPIs and performance reviews are part of the equation, but they soon realize that much of their success depends on how well they navigate the social landscape. Identifying mentors, cultivating relationships, and understanding the inner workings of Amazon's vast ecosystem is just as crucial as mastering the technical aspects of the role. The Amazon jungle is vast, and without the right guides, rookies can easily find themselves lost.

Then there are the veterans—the seasoned warriors who have seen the evolution of Amazon from a scrappy startup to a corporate titan. These individuals have survived the highs and lows, the reorgs and pivots, by mastering the unspoken language of the institution. They've seen initiatives rise and fall and witnessed the ebb and flow of trends and strategies. But through it all, they remain the guardians of Amazon's culture, stewards of its enduring ethos.

Vets carry the institutional memory. They know which levers to pull and whose ear to bend when they need to get things done. Their power lies not just in their knowledge but in their networks. They are the connectors, the ones who understand that while the product might be king, the people are the kingdom. In a place as vast as Amazon, it's their social capital that truly moves mountains.

For the vets, the interview process is a different kind of challenge. They are no longer proving their worth in the traditional sense but instead demonstrating how they have grown as leaders. Their interviews are a dance of finesse and foresight, subtly shifting the focus from what they've done to who they've become. Success isn't just about being a cog in the machine but about shaping the machinery itself. And they understand that, in a company as complex as Amazon, the ability to influence is often more important than the ability to execute.

Caught in the crossfire between rookies and vets are the in-betweens. These individuals exist in a state of perpetual transition—neither the fresh faces of the rookies nor the seasoned hands of the vets. They are the navigators of change, constantly adapting to the shifting tides of Amazon's priorities and projects.

The in-betweens are the ones who have enough experience to understand the system but are still hungry enough to climb higher. They've moved past the initial learning curve but haven't yet reached the point where they can rely solely on their networks. In interviews, the in-betweens must tread carefully, balancing the enthusiasm of the rookies with the strategic wisdom of the vets. They understand that change is constant, and that adaptability is their greatest asset.

Their journey is about finding their place within Amazon's sprawling ecosystem, carving out a niche that leverages both their skills and their relationships. Networking becomes a strategic endeavor, and they cultivate alliances across teams and departments. The in-betweens are the bridge builders, the ones who weave together the disparate threads of Amazon's vast tapestry.

At the end of the day, Amazon, like any corporate entity, thrives on its people. It's a place where innovation is fueled by collaboration, where culture is shaped not just by policies but by the people who embody them. The mythos of meritocracy is tempered by the reality of relationships, and those who rise to the top do so not just on the strength of their ideas but on the strength of their networks.

In the grand theater of corporate life, Amazon is no different from any other stage. The rookies, vets, and in-betweens each play their parts, contributing to the ever-evolving narrative. They learn that while knowledge opens the door, it's who you know that gets you through the hallway and into the room where it happens.

As companies scale, they face a delicate balancing act: maintaining a cohesive culture while allowing room for individual creativity and growth. Amazon's interview process, with its focus on leadership principles, aims to preserve the company's ethos while bringing in fresh perspectives. Yet, the real challenge comes after the hire. How do you ensure that newcomers—whether rookies, vets, or in-betweens—buy into the culture without stifling their individuality?

At Amazon, this balance is achieved by fostering a dynamic interplay between structure and flexibility. The leadership principles provide the structure, the guiding star that aligns everyone's efforts. But within that framework, there is room for individuals to express their creativity, take ownership of their projects, and drive innovation.

As the company grows, so does the challenge of keeping employees engaged with the core values and cultural ethos. Veterans play a crucial role in this by mentoring newcomers and passing on the institutional knowledge that has kept Amazon thriving. But it's not just about the veterans. The in-betweens, with their fresh perspective and understanding of the company's evolving needs, are equally important in driving change and keeping the culture relevant.

The real danger lies in complacency. When employees—whether rookies, vets, or in-betweens—start coasting, the culture begins to erode. Amazon combats this by ensuring that each hire raises the bar for the entire organization. The focus is on continuous improvement, on staying curious, and on always striving to deliver results. It's this relentless pursuit of excellence that keeps Amazon's culture alive and thriving.

In the end, Amazon's success lies in its ability to balance culture and individuality. The leadership principles provide the foundation, but it's the people—the rookies, the vets, and the in-betweens—who drive the company forward. By fostering a culture of trust, ownership, and customer obsession, Amazon ensures that its employees are not just meeting expectations but exceeding them. And in this dance of corporate life, it's the balance between culture and individuality that keeps the music playing.

WHAT I LEARNED:

1. **Rookies**: Newcomers at Amazon must quickly adapt to a rigorous interview process that probes for alignment with Amazon's Leadership Principles. Storytelling and networking are critical to their success in navigating Amazon's complex social and professional ecosystem.
2. **Vets**: Veterans at Amazon are the culture bearers, shaping the company through their vast experience and networks. Their success relies on influence and knowledge of the inner workings of the company, ensuring that Amazon's culture remains intact as it grows.
3. **In-Betweens**: These individuals balance the enthusiasm of the rookies with the wisdom of the vets. Their role is to adapt to constant change and build bridges between departments, navigating Amazon's ecosystem with adaptability and strategic networking.

4. **Unseen Reality**: Success at Amazon, like in most corporations, is as much about relationships as it is about technical skills. Networks and social capital often play a pivotal role in advancing one's career within the company.

5. **Balance of Culture and Individuality**: Amazon fosters a culture that thrives on structure, trust, and leadership principles while encouraging individual creativity. Maintaining this balance is key to keeping the company's ethos strong as it scales.

6. **Battle for Engagement**: As Amazon grows, maintaining employee engagement and cultural alignment is crucial. Continuous improvement and ensuring that each hire raises the bar are core strategies to keep the culture alive and thriving.

CHAPTER 10

THE GLOBAL DANCE – ADAPTING TO CULTURAL DIFFERENCES IN THE HIRING PROCESS

> *"It is not our differences that divide us. It is our inability to recognize, accept, and celebrate those differences."*
> — *Audre Lorde*

*T*he world is a vast mosaic of cultures, each with its own rhythm and rules. At Amazon, a global titan in innovation, the challenge of building teams across borders requires more than just a standard process. It's about understanding the unique cultural nuances that shape how people work, communicate, and make decisions. Having worked across various regions—from the bustling streets of London to the wide expanses of Australia—I've seen firsthand that success lies in adapting to these differences while holding steadfast to core values like trust and delivering results. This chapter delves into the intricacies of managing global teams and highlights how embracing cultural nuances in the hiring process can build stronger, more cohesive teams.

Cultural awareness is crucial when managing a global team. It's more than just knowing time zones or different work holidays. It's about grasping the unspoken rules that influence behavior and decision-making. In different regions, the approach to work and communication varies greatly, and failing to adapt to these differences can hinder success. Whether you're interviewing a candidate from the UK, France, or Australia, you must adjust your methods to align with local customs.

For example, in the UK, conversations often start with small talk about the weather, and patience is valued in the interview process. In France, intellectual discussions might dominate the conversation, while in Australia, knowing the difference between their football codes (NRL and AFL) could build rapport. In Germany, precision is key, and efficiency is highly prized. Each region offers its own set of expectations, and understanding these cultural norms fosters a more effective hiring process and workplace environment.

While understanding culture is vital, the core of global business remains centered on two key aspects: earning trust and delivering results. Trust is built differently across cultures. In some regions, trust is earned over time through consistent performance and respect for local customs. In others, a transparent and direct approach fosters quicker trust-building. Regardless of location, leaders must demonstrate that they value the unique contributions of their global team members.

However, delivering results remains a universal language. No matter the cultural backdrop, results matter, and success is ultimately measured by the tangible outcomes you produce. Translating strategic plans into real-world impact is what solidifies trust and credibility across borders.

Effective communication is the glue that holds global teams together. In the UK, where understatement reigns, subtle and diplomatic language works best, while in Spain, a more passionate and open style of communication is embraced. In Germany, directness and clarity are appreciated, and in Australia, the laid-back yet competitive tone requires a careful balance between humor and seriousness.

Understanding these communication styles allows leaders to tailor their messages to different audiences, ensuring they resonate. The ability to read the room, adjust tone, and use appropriate cultural references is critical when navigating the complexities of managing international teams.

Creating a team that spans continents and cultures requires more than just hiring the right people—it demands fostering unity and collaboration. This can be achieved by celebrating cultural differences and encouraging cross-cultural interactions. By actively promoting a diverse set of voices, global leaders can create an environment where innovation thrives.

A cohesive global team doesn't simply tolerate diversity; it leverages it as a source of strength. Open dialogue, shared goals, and mutual respect are essential to fostering a sense of belonging within such teams. By valuing diverse perspectives and experiences, you create a fertile ground for creativity and high performance.

In global business, maintaining a consistent set of leadership principles is essential. However, to successfully lead across borders, you must adapt to the local cultural nuances and embrace the diversity of your team. By fostering trust, delivering results, and communicating effectively, you can build a cohesive global team that is not only culturally aware but also highly innovative and driven toward success.

Understanding cultural differences isn't just a courtesy—it's a necessity in navigating the complexities of global business. And while your leadership principles can remain consistent, how you apply them must adapt to the cultural context in which you're operating. In the end, it's about blending structure with flexibility, consistency with adaptability, and vision with empathy.

WHAT I LEARNED:

1. **Embrace Cultural Differences:** Whether it's the UK's pub culture or Italy's family-oriented values, cultural awareness is critical in building effective global teams. Leaders must adapt their management style to respect these local nuances, fostering trust and collaboration.

2. **Maintain Core Principles but Be Flexible:** While leadership principles like customer obsession and delivering results remain the same across the board, you must adapt your approach to fit the local cultural context. Core values can stay consistent, but how they are communicated and applied may need to be modified.

3. **Earning Trust Takes Time:** Trust is the backbone of any successful team, but it's built differently across cultures. In countries where trust is earned slowly, patience and transparency are critical. In other regions, delivering results consistently can help accelerate trust-building.

4. **Tailor Your Communication Style:** Understanding the communication preferences of different cultures will help you deliver feedback and motivate your team effectively.

While direct feedback may be appreciated in Germany, a more nuanced approach may be needed in other cultures like Japan or Italy.

5. **Leverage Diversity as a Strength**: A truly global team celebrates its diversity. By encouraging open dialogue and respecting cultural differences, leaders can foster an environment of creativity and innovation that draws on a broad range of perspectives.

6. **Be Mindful of Local Issues**: Acknowledging local customs and addressing region-specific concerns is key. A one-size-fits-all global agenda often doesn't translate well—like pushing an American-centric movement such as Black Lives Matter in Australia where Indigenous rights are a more pertinent issue. Adapting to local concerns shows that you understand and respect the context in which your team operates.

7. **Continuous Adaptation Is Key**: The global business environment is dynamic, and successful leaders are those who continuously adapt. Whether it's changing your approach based on regional needs or fostering stronger connections through a better understanding of cultural contexts, the ability to evolve is crucial.

CHAPTER 11

OUT OF THE MACHINE – REFLECTING ON A DECADE OF AMAZONIAN ALCHEMY

> *"Do not go where the path may lead; go instead where there is no path and leave a trail."*
> — *Ralph Waldo Emerson*

*J*t's been quite the journey—a path that took me from the misty streets of Seattle to the sun-drenched boulevards of Los Angeles, across the Atlantic to the historic lanes of London, and finally to the bustling harbors of Sydney. Over a decade at Amazon, I experienced the transformation of a company once seen as an underdog into the corporate juggernaut it is today. Through countless interviews, interactions, and navigating the ever-shifting landscapes of the cities we called home, the experience of being part of Amazon shaped a decade of learning and leadership.

In 2011, Amazon wasn't the global giant it is today. In Seattle, we operated like a band of rebels, experimenting with ideas, iterating on failures, and striving for success in a culture not yet fully formed. Amazon's growth felt organic, with a focus on innovation, a start-up mentality, and a relentless push to turn ideas into reality. Seattle was our proving ground, a place where scrappy determination collided with big dreams.

When I first joined, Amazon was still expanding its wings. It had a solid foundation, but no one could have predicted the heights it would eventually reach. We weren't polished or perfect; we were a collection of passionate individuals who believed in the power of technology to disrupt industries. Each day, we walked into work, knowing that we were building something bigger than ourselves. Every decision, from the smallest feature update to the launch of major new initiatives, was driven by one guiding force: customer obsession.

The Bar Raiser program, a mechanism to ensure high hiring standards, was still new, and being a Bar Raiser meant finding those rare talents who could thrive in ambiguity. It wasn't just about hiring people to fill roles but hiring those who would shape the future, contributing to the evolving culture. This program wasn't just an internal audit; it was an act of curation, sculpting the workforce of a company that, at the time, was still growing into its identity.

Seattle, in those days, was the crucible where Amazon's ethos—customer obsession, delivering results, and ownership—was tested and refined. We weren't yet cool, but we were on the brink of something remarkable. There was a feeling that we were all part of an experiment, one in which success wasn't guaranteed, but the journey itself held immense value. The idea of innovation wasn't just something we discussed; it was something we lived. The failures weren't just setbacks; they were vital lessons that propelled us forward.

Moving to Los Angeles felt like entering a different world. LA's creative energy influenced how Amazon operated, especially as it expanded into entertainment and media. Amazon Prime Video was emerging, and the city's blend of tech and entertainment reshaped our approach to hiring. We needed visionaries who could navigate this fast-evolving world, individuals with both technical expertise and creativity.

Los Angeles, known for its ability to reinvent itself, became a proving ground for Amazon's entertainment ambitions. The launch of Amazon Studios, Prime Video, and our foray into Hollywood weren't just side projects—they were pivotal moves that defined the future of the company. We were no longer confined to selling products online; we were becoming storytellers and content creators.

Interviews in Los Angeles were different. We weren't just looking for people who could build things—we needed people who could imagine new worlds. Creativity was at a premium, and we sought out those who could blend technical skills with an artistic sensibility. The balance between innovation and execution was critical. The people we hired had to be able to think in cinematic terms while also understanding the technology that would bring those ideas to life.

Our team was a mosaic of talent drawn from diverse backgrounds, each bringing a unique perspective to the table. We were no longer just techies in hoodies; we were visionaries in the making, reshaping the narrative of what Amazon could be. We saw firsthand how different the business was becoming. Los Angeles wasn't just about scaling operations—it was about defining the future of media and entertainment. And as we grew, so did our understanding of what it took to succeed in an industry driven by both creativity and disruption.

Crossing the Atlantic to London was a whole new challenge. This city, steeped in tradition, made us balance innovation with respect for history. Here, I saw how important it was to learn the subtleties of different cultures, particularly when it came to leadership and hiring.

In London, it wasn't just about what you could do—it was about how you presented yourself. Interviews here had an extra layer of complexity, requiring a level of cultural dexterity that wasn't always necessary in other locations. It wasn't enough to have great ideas; you had to know how to frame those ideas within the context of the local market. We found ourselves hiring not just for skill but for adaptability and an understanding of the British mindset.

Interviews in London required a different approach. Candidates were often more nuanced, and the culture valued diplomacy and thoughtful engagement. We learned to be more patient and more considerate of the slow-build trust that defined British business relationships. It was no longer just about moving fast and breaking things—it was about understanding the delicate balance between speed and sustainability.

In London, we were challenged to think more globally and to operate with an awareness of the broader implications of our work. Our mindset expanded beyond the transactional, focusing more on relationship-building and long-term innovation. London taught us that sometimes, slowing down to listen and engage deeply with the local culture could lead to more profound results.

Sydney, the final stop in this journey, represented a new frontier where Amazon was no longer an outsider but a trusted name. Sydney's vibrant entrepreneurial spirit fueled Amazon's ambitions, and my experience as a Bar Raiser evolved. Here, I saw firsthand the maturation of Amazon's interview process—where the goal shifted from identifying talent to nurturing it.

Sydney wasn't just about expanding geographically; it was about redefining what success looked like for Amazon on a global scale. The market was different, the challenges were unique, and the opportunities were immense. We had to be more strategic and more focused on long-term growth. This was a place where Amazon had the opportunity to learn from its mistakes, to adapt and evolve in ways that weren't always possible in more established markets.

As a Bar Raiser in Sydney, I saw the impact of cultural awareness on hiring decisions. We weren't just hiring for technical ability; we were hiring for a cultural fit that could bridge the gap between local sensibilities and Amazon's global ethos. The people we brought on board needed to understand the unique dynamics of the Australian market while also being able to innovate on a global scale.

Sydney taught us the value of adaptability and resilience. It reinforced the notion that while the journey may change, the core principles remain: Earn trust, deliver results, and always raise the bar. The city itself mirrored this philosophy, blending a laid-back attitude with a fierce drive to succeed. And in that sense, Sydney became the perfect metaphor for Amazon's own journey—constantly evolving yet always grounded in the pursuit of excellence.

Throughout my time at Amazon, I had the privilege of witnessing leadership in its many forms. Jeff Bezos, the visionary founder, set the tone with a relentless focus on long-term thinking and customer obsession. Jeff Wilke, the operations expert, refined Amazon's logistics and efficiency, creating the backbone that supports its vast network. Andy Jassy, who pioneered AWS, embodied the future of cloud computing and technology.

Each leader brought a unique flavor to Amazon, each navigating the company through different phases of growth. Success, while often measured by numbers, was ultimately about the transformations these leaders guided. From Jeff Bezos's early vision of Amazon as "the everything store" to Andy Jassy's focus on cloud computing, each leader played a pivotal role in shaping the company's trajectory.

Jeff Wilke, in particular, was instrumental in taking the raw innovation of the early days and turning it into something scalable. Under his leadership, we built the systems that allowed Amazon to grow into the logistics powerhouse it is today. His focus on operational excellence created the foundation upon which Amazon's entire business model rests.

Andy Jassy, now at the helm, represents the future—a focus on technology and services that transcend traditional retail boundaries. He's the one leading Amazon into the world of cloud computing, artificial intelligence, and beyond. With AWS, Amazon has positioned itself as a leader in a field that didn't even exist a decade ago, and Jassy's leadership reflects the company's ongoing commitment to innovation.

As Amazon continues to evolve, the seeds of the next wave of innovation are being sown. Whether in artificial intelligence, fintech, or entirely new sectors, the next phase will require continued adaptation, creativity, and leadership.

The world is changing faster than ever, and Amazon's ability to stay ahead of the curve will depend on its willingness to embrace new ideas and new ways of working. We've already seen the company expand beyond its original remit into areas like cloud computing, artificial intelligence, and media. The question now is, where will Amazon go next? The possibilities are endless, but the key to success will be maintaining the same customer-centric focus that got the company this far.

WHAT I LEARNED:

1. **The Importance of the Bar Raiser Program:** As a Bar Raiser, I saw how maintaining high hiring standards shaped Amazon's culture and ensured that every hire was not just competent but exceptional. This program, which can be adapted to other organizations, is a way to preserve quality and build long-term success.

2. **Global Cultural Awareness:** Whether in the U.S., the U.K., or Australia, understanding and adapting to cultural nuances in hiring and leadership was crucial. Being aware of local values and traditions builds trust and allows for more meaningful collaboration.

3. **Innovation Through Collaboration:** The success of Amazon lies not only in its ability to innovate but in its ability to foster collaboration across diverse teams and regions. This global perspective ensures that innovation is not confined to one place but thrives in every corner of the world.

4. **Adaptability and Resilience:** The ability to adapt to changing circumstances, both in the market and within the company, was key to Amazon's growth. From shifting

priorities in hiring to navigating new industries, resilience and flexibility were critical.

5. **Customer Obsession as the North Star:** Throughout every city and phase of Amazon's journey, customer obsession remained the central pillar of success. This principle—working backward from the customer—ensured that every decision, product, and initiative was grounded in delivering value to the end user.

6. **Leadership Styles for Different Eras:** Whether you're an operator, visionary, or pioneer, leadership at Amazon reflected the needs of each era. As the company evolved, so did its leaders, guiding it through different phases with distinct styles but always grounded in core principles.

CHAPTER 12

TRANSLATING AMAZON'S LESSONS TO YOUR JOURNEY

> *"Experience without theory is blind, but theory without experience is mere intellectual play."*
> *— Immanuel Kant*

The road from startup to empire is paved with hard-earned lessons, trials faced, and wisdom gained along the way. This is a journey that Amazon, from its humble beginnings as an online bookseller to its meteoric rise as a global behemoth, navigated with a unique blend of audacity, resilience, and relentless innovation. As we reflect on the key lessons from Amazon's story, there are invaluable insights that can be translated into any entrepreneurial endeavor, guiding both leaders and organizations on their own paths to success. This chapter is about taking those insights—adapting them, making them your own, and applying them to your journey.

Change is the only constant in the world of business, and those who fear it often stagnate. At Amazon, change is not simply tolerated; it is relentlessly pursued, and that pursuit of improvement fuels innovation, drives growth, and ensures the company's relevance in an ever-evolving market. This commitment to change underpins Amazon's success, serving as a powerful reminder that adaptability is more than just reacting to disruption. It's about seeing the writing on the wall before others, positioning yourself to be ahead of the curve.

One of the keys to Amazon's success has been its ability to pivot quickly and decisively. For example, when Amazon first launched its marketplace, it was primarily focused on books. However, it didn't take long for leadership to realize that there were broader opportunities to capitalize on. By pivoting away from its core product line and diversifying its offerings, Amazon became the "everything store" it is today. This ability to shift focus, embrace new opportunities, and adapt to market trends is what enabled Amazon to go from an online bookstore to a global tech giant.

But adaptability isn't just about shifting products; it's about embracing new realities, even when they challenge your current assumptions. Amazon's venture into cloud computing with AWS is a prime example of a business completely transforming itself to adapt to a new opportunity. Initially, AWS was born out of Amazon's need to manage its own infrastructure, but it quickly evolved into a massive business that now generates more profit than its retail arm.

AWS represents a crucial lesson for any business: sometimes, the biggest opportunities are hidden in the operational pain points you may face. By solving its own infrastructure problems, Amazon stumbled upon a business opportunity that revolutionized the tech industry. AWS is now the backbone for countless businesses, providing cloud computing services to enterprises and startups alike. This wasn't part of Amazon's original business model, but it became one of its most significant ventures because of Amazon's willingness to explore and embrace the potential of what was originally seen as an internal solution.

Foster a culture of adaptability and reinvention. Encourage your team to explore new ideas, challenge old assumptions, and think beyond the present. The world is changing rapidly, and businesses that refuse to adapt will find themselves left behind. The most successful companies aren't the ones that stick to their original plan; they're the ones that are willing to pivot when the opportunity presents itself.

Metrics are the foundation of data-driven decision-making, and at Amazon, metrics are treated with almost religious reverence. The company thrives on data, and the ability to dissect, analyze, and derive insights from that data is one of the reasons for its success. Metrics provide the clarity needed to see the truth of a situation—whether it's a product that isn't performing as expected, a process that's costing more than it should, or a market opportunity that's ripe for the taking.

At Amazon, decisions are rarely made without first consulting the data. The company's famous "two-pizza teams"—small, agile teams that can be fed with two pizzas— are given the autonomy to act quickly, but they are always held accountable through metrics. Whether it's tracking customer satisfaction, delivery times, or operational efficiency, metrics are baked into the DNA of every Amazon team.

Develop a metrics-driven culture in your organization. Define KPIs that align with your business goals and ensure every team member understands how their performance is measured. Metrics provide a clear path to improvement, allowing you to spot inefficiencies, evaluate progress, and make informed decisions that drive growth.

While data-driven decision-making is powerful, it's important to remember that metrics are only as good as the questions you ask. One of Amazon's most valuable lessons is that not all metrics are created equal. Focusing on vanity metrics—numbers that look good on paper but don't actually drive meaningful results—can lead businesses astray.

Consider a startup that is focused on acquiring as many users as possible without paying attention to user retention or engagement. The number of users may be skyrocketing, but if those users aren't sticking around, the business is headed for trouble. Amazon's obsession with data ensures that every team focuses on the metrics that truly matter—metrics that reflect real customer behavior and long-term value.

In your business, be vigilant about the metrics you track. Ensure that your data is telling you something meaningful, not just something that looks impressive on a graph.

Amazon's love affair with data doesn't diminish its understanding of the human element. While metrics drive decision-making, Amazon's leadership understands that behind every data point is a human being—a customer, an employee, or a partner. That's why customer obsession is such a crucial part of Amazon's ethos. Every metric must ultimately serve the customer experience.

For your journey, the lesson here is simple: metrics should be used to inform decisions, not dictate them. Always keep the human side of business in mind. Whether you're developing a new product, launching a marketing campaign, or making decisions about company culture, ask yourself how those decisions will impact your customers and your team.

In a company like Amazon, where tens of thousands of interviews happen each year, you might think efficiency would come before connection. But one of the most powerful lessons I learned as a Bar Raiser is that there's no substitute for genuine human connection during an interview.

"Never interview with a laptop" is not just practical advice; it's a philosophy that underlines how important it is to truly engage with people. Typing away on your laptop during an interview creates an impersonal and disconnected atmosphere. Candidates feel like they're just another name on a list, and you miss out on critical nuances that could indicate whether they're the right fit for your organization.

When I was conducting interviews at Amazon, I would always set my laptop aside. I would walk into the room with questions prepared on paper but wouldn't let them bind me to a script. Instead, I would focus on the candidate, listen intently, and let the conversation guide me. Some of the best insights came from unscripted moments when a candidate opened up about a challenge they faced or a project they were passionate about.

By interviewing without a laptop, you create space for genuine conversation. You foster an environment where candidates feel heard and valued, and in return, you gain deeper insights into who they are—not just what they can do.

At Amazon, the hiring process is rigorous for a reason. The company's Bar Raiser program ensures that every hire is not just good enough for the role but has the potential to raise the overall performance of the team. This intentionality in hiring is a crucial part of Amazon's success. They don't just look for people who can do the job; they look for people who can elevate the work of those around them.

In your business, applying the Bar Raiser mindset means being extremely selective in your hiring process. Don't settle for someone who meets the minimum qualifications. Instead, look for individuals who will challenge the status quo, bring fresh perspectives, and push your team to new heights. It may take longer to fill the role, but the payoff will be worth it when you have a team that consistently outperforms expectations.

One of Amazon's most innovative processes is the Working Backwards method. This approach ensures that every project starts with a clear understanding of what success looks like from the customer's perspective. It all begins with writing a press release or a Dear Customer Letter—long before a product or service is built. This document outlines exactly what the product does, why it matters, and how it will impact the customer.

By focusing on the end goal from the outset, the Working Backwards method ensures that the customer remains at the heart of every decision. Teams use this process to clearly articulate the value of a product, ensuring alignment across the board.

For your journey, adopting this method means thinking critically about what success looks like. Start every project by writing down what the final result should be. How will your product or service improve the customer's life? What problems will it solve? Why should they care? These questions will help you stay focused on what really matters and avoid getting bogged down in irrelevant details.

Translating Amazon's lessons to your journey is not about imitation—it's about adaptation. These principles, honed over decades of experimentation and growth, can guide any business, whether you're a startup or an established enterprise. The key is to take these insights and apply them in a way that aligns with your unique goals, challenges, and vision.

WHAT I LEARNED:

1. **Embrace Change and Adaptability:** Foster a culture that thrives on change, encourages experimentation, and empowers teams to innovate. The ability to pivot and adapt to new realities is a key driver of success.
2. **Harness the Power of Metrics:** Build a data-driven organization where decisions are informed by clear, actionable insights. Track progress rigorously and ensure your metrics align with your long-term goals.
3. **Engage Deeply in Interviews:** Put away the laptop and have real conversations with candidates. Build rapport, ask thoughtful questions, and listen for the qualities that will help your business grow.
4. **Adopt the Working Backwards Process:** Start with the customer and work backward to build solutions. Use tools like the Press Release method to ensure that every initiative is focused on delivering real value.
5. **Build Teams with Intent**: Set a high bar for hiring and ensure that every new team member not only meets your current needs but has the potential to elevate the organization.

6. **Remember the Human Side:** Metrics are powerful, but they must serve the human side of your business. Keep customers, employees, and partners in mind with every decision you make.

CHAPTER 13

FOLLOW YOUR TALENT, NOT YOUR PASSION

"Knowledge and error flow from the same mental sources; only success can tell one from the other."
— *Ernst Mach*

*L*et's dismantle the myth once and for all: "Follow your passion" is a dangerously oversimplified mantra sold by those who've rarely grappled with the complexities of real-world success. Passion doesn't pay the bills. It doesn't solve hard problems. And it certainly doesn't build careers. What does? Talent. Raw, refined, and relentless talent, developed through discipline, honed by failure, and proven by results.

Passion without substance is like setting out on a road trip with no map and no fuel—it's bound to fizzle out. Talent, on the other hand, is the vehicle that keeps moving, even when the road is uncertain and the destination unclear.

Passion feels good. It's intoxicating, seductive even. But let's be honest—it's fleeting. Passion can get you started, but when the novelty wears off or the challenges start piling up, it's talent that keeps you in the game. Talent is what helps you solve the problems that passion alone can't.

At Amazon, passion was never the litmus test for hiring or success. Instead, the focus was on results. It wasn't enough to be passionate about innovation or obsessed with the company's mission—you had to deliver. You had to demonstrate skill, resilience, and the ability to move the needle. Passion could be a bonus, but talent was the currency that mattered.

Here's an example: A colleague of mine was deeply passionate about design. They were creative, brimming with ideas, and had an infectious enthusiasm for their craft. But passion didn't help when they struggled to meet deadlines or translate their vision into actionable deliverables. Another teammate, less outwardly passionate but highly skilled at execution, quietly outperformed. The lesson was clear: while passion is admirable, it's talent that drives impact.

Ernst Mach's observation that "knowledge and error flow from the same mental sources; only success can tell one from the other" hits at the core of why talent matters. It's not about starting with all the answers—it's about developing the ability to identify and correct errors through experience and perseverance. Success clarifies what works and what doesn't, and talent is the mechanism through which this clarity is achieved.

When I started at Amazon, I wasn't passionate about logistics, data analysis, or scaling operations. However, I was good at solving complex problems, working cross-functionally, and simplifying complicated ones. These weren't glamorous skills, but they were invaluable. Over time, I leaned into them, refining my ability to execute at scale. The more I succeeded, the more rewarding the work became—and that's when passion began to emerge.

Here's the truth no one tells you: passion often follows success, not the other way around. When you excel at something, when you see the tangible results of your efforts, it's hard not to feel passionate about it. Success breeds satisfaction, which in turn fuels motivation and excitement.

Talent isn't a magical gift bestowed upon a lucky few. It's a combination of skills, discipline, and execution—qualities that can be cultivated. Unlike passion, which can be fleeting and whimsical, talent is dependable. It scales with you, grows through repetition, and becomes sharper with every challenge you face.

At Amazon, this philosophy was reinforced in every Bar Raiser interview I conducted. Candidates who excelled weren't the ones who waxed poetic about their passion for the company; they were the ones who could articulate their track record of solving problems, delivering results, and growing from setbacks. They didn't just *feel* passionate—they were competent, reliable, and adaptable.

The problem with passion is that it often blinds you to reality. People chase passions that feel good but don't align with their strengths, market demand, or the skills they've developed. They pour energy into endeavors that are exciting at first but fizzle out when the going gets tough.

Consider this: How many aspiring musicians, athletes, or entrepreneurs have burned out because they pursued their passion without cultivating the necessary skills to succeed? Talent requires a foundation of competence and discipline. Passion alone can't sustain you through the inevitable obstacles.

WHAT I LEARNED:

1. **Identify Your Strengths**: What do you excel at naturally? What skills do you bring to the table that others value? Pay attention to what people consistently praise you for or seek your help with. These are your raw talents.

2. **Double Down on Development**: Talent isn't static—it's a muscle that grows with use. Invest time in honing your strengths through practice, education, and real-world application. Surround yourself with mentors and peers who challenge you to improve.

3. **Solve Real Problems**: Passion often chases dreams; talent solves problems. Look for areas where your skills can make an impact. The more problems you solve, the more value you create—and the more rewarding the work becomes.

4. **Measure Success by Results**: Passion feels good, but results pay the bills. Focus on outcomes, not just effort. Ask yourself: What have I delivered? What difference have I made? Let these results guide your path.

5. **Let Passion Follow**: Passion isn't irrelevant, but it's a byproduct of doing meaningful, successful work. When you see the impact of your efforts—whether it's a project completed, a customer satisfied, or a team inspired—passion will naturally follow.

CHAPTER 14

WALTZING WITH THE ABYSS – LESSONS IN RUTHLESS SURVIVAL

"Man is the cruelest animal."
— *Friedrich Nietzsche*

The corporate world is often framed as a land of opportunity—a utopia of innovation, collaboration, and meritocracy. But behind the shiny facades of glass-walled boardrooms and perfectly worded mission statements lies a battlefield. It's a theater where ambition masquerades as camaraderie, where egos collide in a relentless quest for power, and where survival often depends on your ability to navigate the shadows.

For more than 12 years, I lived and worked in this world, from Seattle to Sydney. What I learned wasn't in handbooks or onboarding sessions—it was extracted through gritted teeth and sleepless nights, in the trenches of manipulation, betrayal, and survival.

This chapter isn't a cautionary tale or a guide to avoiding the pitfalls of corporate life. It's a reckoning—a hard look at the realities of thriving in a system that rewards ruthlessness and punishes integrity.

From the start, the rules of the game are unwritten but painfully clear. You pour your heart into leading high-performing teams, exceed expectations, and imagine recognition and respect will follow. Instead, you hear whispers in meetings:

- ◈ "You're too smart for your own good. You make me look stupid."
- ◈ "Your achievements will be reassigned. Someone else needs this win."

These words aren't just insults; they're systemic warnings. Merit isn't the currency here—optics and alliances are. It's a lesson learned through humiliation and frustration: the most competent players aren't always the winners. Often, the victors are those who understand the subtle choreography of politics.

One of the first truths I learned was that lies aren't just tolerated in corporate environments—they're rewarded. People with silver tongues, adept at spinning half-truths and taking credit for work they barely touched, are often celebrated as visionaries. Meanwhile, those who insist on integrity are sidelined, branded as "difficult" or "too rigid."

I saw people claw their way up the corporate ladder on the backs of others, stealing ideas and credit with breathtaking audacity. Meetings became arenas where deception wasn't just common—it was an art form. Watching this unfold was both infuriating and absurd.

Meritocracy is a myth. Promotions and opportunities often depend more on alliances and appearances than results. This isn't personal; it's strategy. Once you accept this, you can focus on resilience rather than fairness.

The corporate grind slowly chips away at your confidence. It whispers doubts into your mind: *Am I good enough? Am I even capable?* Refuse to let these doubts take root. Confidence is your strongest defense against a culture designed to erode it.

When your integrity or future is at stake, documentation is your best ally. Keep records of decisions, conversations, and outcomes. Facts are your armor in a world of whispered accusations and selective memory.

Not every hill is worth dying on. Some fights—no matter how justified—will drain your energy without yielding results. Learn to disengage from toxic people and situations. Sometimes, the best move is to let their chaos consume itself.

Amidst the predators, there are a few rare individuals who refuse to play dirty. These allies are invaluable. Build relationships with those who see through the charade, who value integrity, and who remind you that not everyone has traded their soul for success.

Corporate culture loves to sell the idea of success as climbing a ladder, one rung at a time. But that ladder is often propped up by mediocrity and built on a foundation of politics. Real success doesn't mean reaching the top of their game—it means defining your own game.

- ◈ Success is walking away with your dignity intact.
- ◈ Success is refusing to let their chaos shape your identity.
- ◈ Success is knowing when to leave a toxic environment.

I remember one absurd moment vividly. I opposed a promotion for someone who was wholly unfit for the role, listing specific reasons why they lacked the competence to succeed. They were promoted anyway, and their lies were dressed up as charm. It was maddening, but it also underscored a critical truth: winning their game isn't the point. Winning yours is.

The ultimate power move isn't climbing higher—it's knowing when to walk away. Staying in a toxic environment doesn't make you strong; it makes you complicit. Leaving on your own terms is an act of defiance. It's reclaiming your narrative and choosing your well-being over a system that will never choose you.

Walking away doesn't mean failure. It means freedom. It means choosing to stop dancing with shadows and starting to live in the light.

Nietzsche's warning is one I carried with me every day: *Stare too long into the abyss, and it stares back into you.* It's easy to let the culture shape you, to adopt its ruthlessness as a survival mechanism. But the true battle isn't against the politics or the lies—it's against becoming what you hate.

Survival isn't just about enduring; it's about maintaining your integrity in a world that rewards duplicity. It's about resisting the temptation to become the very thing you despise. In the end, the abyss may stare back, but it doesn't define you. You define yourself by how you choose to navigate the chaos, by the battles you fight, and by the ones you walk away from. Survival is about more than endurance—it's about transformation. And in the face of relentless cruelty, it's about holding onto the humanity they tried to strip away.

WHAT I LEARNED:

1. **The Game Is Cruel, but You Don't Have to Be:** The corporate jungle thrives on ruthlessness, but you can choose empathy. Success is sweeter when achieved on your terms, not theirs.

2. **Integrity Is Your Anchor:** The world may chip away at your confidence, but your integrity is non-negotiable. Guard it fiercely.

3. **Redefine Winning:** Don't let others define success for you. Define it for yourself and pursue it with purpose.

4. **Know When to Leave:** Staying isn't strength; it's surrender. Walking away is the ultimate act of courage.

CHAPTER 15

MODELS AS TOOLS – NAVIGATING INNOVATION WITHOUT ILLUSIONS

"To present phenomena without demanding
the full truth is itself a form of respect
for reality."
— Bas C. van Fraassen

*I*n the high-speed world of corporate innovation, there's a temptation to believe in grand, sweeping truths— the kind of insights that promise to unravel every mystery and solve every problem. But the real world is messy, and the tools we use to navigate it are often messier still. Models, algorithms, frameworks—they're not monuments to eternal truths. They're wrenches and screwdrivers, duct tape and zip ties. Imperfect, makeshift, but utterly essential.

This is the lesson I learned over twelve years at Amazon. It's a place where pragmatism trumps perfection, where tools are valued not for their elegance but for their utility. Models at Amazon weren't revered like sacred texts. They were created, tested, broken, and rebuilt. They weren't flawless; they were functional. And that made all the difference.

Consider the time we rolled out a new advertising algorithm. The goal was ambitious: predict customer behavior with uncanny accuracy, driving clicks and conversions like never before. And for a while, it worked—or at least it seemed to. But then came the hiccups: edge cases the algorithm couldn't handle, assumptions that didn't hold up in the wild.

Did we treat the algorithm like a failed prophecy? Did we mourn its imperfections? No. We treated it like a hammer that couldn't drive in every nail. Useful in some contexts, useless in others. The solution wasn't to abandon it but to iterate—to learn from its limitations and make it better.

That's the thing about models. They're not about uncovering universal truths. They're about creating something that works, something that can survive contact with the chaos of reality. And when they don't work, you don't panic—you pivot.

One of Amazon's most valuable cultural traits was its ruthless pragmatism. Decisions weren't made based on gut feelings or lofty visions. They were made based on data, on measurable outcomes, on what could be tested and verified.

I remember sitting in meetings where pet theories—ideas people had clearly become attached to—were dismantled by cold, hard data. It wasn't personal. It wasn't even contentious. The question was never, *"Do we like this idea?"* It was always, *"Does this idea work?"* And if the answer was no, we moved on.

This pragmatism had a cost. There were days when it felt like Amazon's soul had been replaced by spreadsheets and KPIs, when creativity seemed to take a backseat to cold efficiency. But those moments were balanced by the thrill of discovery— the moments when a model exceeded expectations, when a solution emerged from the chaos and delivered real value.

One of my favorite projects at Amazon was designing a system to predict delivery times. It wasn't glamorous, but it was critical. Customers needed accurate delivery estimates, and we needed to provide them.

The first version of the model worked—kind of. It nailed the simple cases but floundered in complex ones. But instead of scrapping it, we treated it like a rough draft. Each iteration brought improvements. Each failure taught us something new. By the end, the model wasn't perfect, but it was good enough to trust.

That word—*trust*—became a guiding principle. Customers didn't care if our models were perfect. They cared that their packages arrived when we said they would. And trust, I realized, wasn't built on theoretical perfection. It was built on reliability and on meeting expectations consistently.

Models teach you humility. They remind you that no matter how much data you collect, no matter how advanced your algorithms, the world will always surprise you. Human behavior, market conditions, unforeseen variables—reality is too complex to be captured fully by any model.

But that's okay. The goal isn't to conquer reality; it's to engage with it. To learn from it. To use the tools, you have to make a tangible difference. Models aren't about achieving perfection. They're about creating utility.

One of the biggest mistakes you can make is falling in love with your models. Treating them as sacred truths instead of functional tools. When you do that, you stop iterating. You stop questioning. You start clinging to something that's no longer serving its purpose.

At Amazon, we knew better. Models were disposable. If they worked, great. If they didn't, we learned why and moved on. This mindset wasn't just practical—it was liberating. It freed us from the pressure to get everything right the first time and allowed us to focus on continuous improvement.

Looking back, I've realized that the models we built at Amazon weren't just tools for business. They were metaphors for how to approach life and work. They taught us to value progress over perfection, to embrace iteration, and to respect the complexity of the world. Models aren't about claiming to know everything. They're about doing the best you can with what you know, while staying open to the possibility that there's always more to learn.

The beauty of models lies in their imperfection. They're not monuments to human ingenuity—they're tools for navigating the unknown. At Amazon, I learned that the best models are the ones that embrace their limitations, that iterate in the face of failure, and that ultimately make life a little easier for the people who rely on them. In the end, the goal isn't to create something perfect. It's to create something that works, something that matters. And that, I believe, is a model worth following.

WHAT I LEARNED:

1. **Treat Models as Tools, Not Truths**: Models are means to an end. Use them to solve problems, but don't expect them to capture the full complexity of the world.
2. **Iterate Relentlessly**: Every failure is an opportunity to learn. Treat your models as rough drafts, and never stop refining them.
3. **Focus on Reliability, Not Perfection**: Trust isn't built on flawless systems. It's built on systems that work well enough to meet expectations consistently.

4. **Respect Reality**: The world is too complex to be fully understood. Approach it with humility, curiosity, and a willingness to adapt.

5. **Let Go When Necessary**: When a model stops working, don't cling to it. Have the courage to move on and build something better.

APPENDIX: WORKING BACKWARD – A CASE STUDY IN MAKING THINGS HAPPEN

> *"The reasonable man adapts himself to the world; the unreasonable one persists in trying to adapt the world to himself. Therefore, all progress depends on the unreasonable man."*
> — *George Bernard Shaw*

*D*uring my time at Amazon, I made it a point to write four to six PR FAQs per year for the Amazon OP1 and OP2 cycles, which is the Amazon planning process. I've probably written between 40 and 60 PR FAQs. Some were met with enthusiasm; others were torn apart, ridiculed, and rejected without a second thought. But that was the process. That was the price of innovation. If you're not writing something people want to tear to shreds, you're probably not pushing hard enough. And yet, among the wreckage, there were the ones that stuck—the ones that led to real products, real innovations, things that never existed before.

In fact, almost every role I had at Amazon wasn't something I was simply handed—I had to write my way into it. My ability to craft a document, make a compelling case, and convince people to take a chance on an idea was how I ended up working across different teams, different countries, and entirely new spaces. Writing wasn't just about putting words on a page; it was about making the case for something that didn't yet exist, then proving why it should.

This is the playbook—not just for getting ideas approved in a massive, established organization but for testing the viability of a new startup concept. Whether you're navigating corporate bureaucracy or trying to figure out if your crazy idea has legs, the key is simple: Fail fast, pivot faster. Most ideas will get shot down. That's expected. But every rejection is an opportunity to refine, adjust, and come back with something better. If you can master that, you won't just get ideas approved—you'll change the game.

STAGE 1: LISTEN

Most people talk too much and listen too little. Your job? Shut up and absorb. Not just the words, but the silences in between. What do people actually need? What problem eats at them in the middle of the night? They won't always tell you outright, but it's there, buried in their choices, in their frustrations, in the things they don't even realize they care about. Your edge is in hearing what others ignore. Answer these questions:

- ◆ Who are you actually building this for?
- ◆ Who are you *not* building this for?
- ◆ Where is the hard data proving this is a problem?
- ◆ Who else should you be talking to?
- ◆ What are the biggest unknowns?

STAGE 2: DEFINE

Don't fall for surface-level problems. The real issues sit underneath, tangled in bad assumptions and lazy thinking. People don't want a better horse; they want a car. Your job is to strip it all down until you hit the truth—because if you're solving the wrong problem, you're just burning time and cash.

Think about these questions:

◈ What patterns are emerging from what you've learned?

◈ Can you sum up the problem like this?

"Today, [customer] has to deal with [problem] every time they [situation]. They need a way to [solution]."

If not, go back and clarify.

STAGE 3: INVENT

Creativity isn't magic—it's taking what exists and pushing it further. Break rules, challenge assumptions, and blow up the status quo. You're not here to make a slightly better version of what already exists. You're here to create something undeniable. Something that shifts the landscape.

◈ How will you generate solutions that don't suck?

◈ Who needs to be involved?

◈ What's already out there, and why isn't it enough?

STAGE 4: REFINE

A great idea means nothing if it's bloated with fluff and nonsense. Cut away the excess. Simplicity isn't about having less—it's about having only what matters. Every extra feature, every extra word, every unnecessary detail is dead weight. The best solutions are clean, sharp, and relentless in their efficiency. Here is what you should consider:

- ❖ Can you explain your idea in 30 seconds?
- ❖ Walk through the customer experience—step by step. Where does it fail?
- ❖ What's the core of this? No fluff, no excess—just the beating heart of the idea.
- ❖ Who is going to help write, review, and challenge this document?

STAGE 5: TEST AND ITERATE

Failure is a given. Get over it. The first version will suck. So will the second. That's how progress works. You test, you break things, you learn, and you adjust. The graveyard is full of people who wanted to be right instead of getting it right. Be ruthless in your iteration. The market doesn't care about your ego—it cares about results. Think about these questions:

- ❖ What assumptions need to be validated first?
- ❖ What's your testing plan?
- ❖ How will you know if it's a success or a disaster?

THE PRESS RELEASE OR DEAR CUSTOMER LETTER: A REALITY CHECK

The Dear Customer Letter is more than a simple announcement—it's a direct conversation with the very people your business serves. It's not about flashy marketing or impersonal press releases; it's about crafting an honest, clear message that connects with the customer on a human level. This approach strips away the corporate jargon and speaks to customers as if they were sitting across the table from you. Whether you're a scrappy startup launching your first product or an established business with decades of history, this letter serves as a reminder of why you exist in the first place: to serve the customer.

At its core, the Dear Customer Letter is a philosophy—a way of thinking that puts your customer at the center of everything you do. It's not just about what you're launching but why it matters to them. You're not speaking to the faceless masses; you're speaking to someone with real needs, frustrations, and hopes. And that's where the magic happens—when you drop the corporate mask and have a real conversation.

Writing one of these forces you to face the truth. If you can't sell it to a future customer in plain language, it's probably not worth doing.

For startups: You're small, you're hungry, and you're looking for that breakthrough. Your customers are taking a chance on something new, something untested. The Dear Customer Letter is your opportunity to reassure them. Be excited, but don't oversell. Be real about the journey and why this product or service is going to change the game for them.

Every sentence should ooze with passion, because if you're not excited, why should they be? Here's your chance to create a personal connection, something that can't be done through traditional marketing alone.

For established businesses: You've already earned their trust—but that doesn't mean you get to rest. The Dear Customer Letter lets you stay fresh, human, and in touch with your audience. It's a chance to keep evolving the relationship with your customers, showing them that even though you're big, you're still thinking about how to make their lives better. Maybe it's a new feature that simplifies an old process or a service that's going to save them time. Either way, the letter reminds your customers why they chose you in the first place and why they should stick with you in the future.

Ultimately, the Dear Customer Letter is a conversation. It's not about bells and whistles or grand proclamations. It's about honesty, clarity, and a shared understanding that your customer is the reason your business exists at all. Whether you're trying to carve out a space in a crowded market or hold onto a hard-earned legacy, this letter is your opportunity to speak directly to the people who matter most—your customers. Keep it real, keep it simple, and, most importantly, keep them at the center of everything you do.

1. Start with the customer's reaction. What will they say when this thing actually works?
2. Kill the corporate jargon. If it sounds like an ad or a TED Talk, start over.
3. Focus on impact—real benefits, not empty hype.
4. Get to the damn point. If the first paragraph doesn't hook them, you've failed.

5. Don't waste words explaining obvious details.
6. Read it out loud. If it sounds fake, it is.
7. Be concise. Every sentence must earn its place.
8. Get an outside perspective. Fresh eyes catch your blind spots.
9. Ditch the marketing fluff—no one believes it.
10. End with action—what's the next step?

FAQS: BECAUSE SOMEONE'S GOING TO ASK ANYWAY

Don't wait for the tough questions—answer them before they're asked. Here are the big ones:

◈ What problem are you solving, and why now?
◈ Why should anyone care?
◈ How is this better than what already exists?
◈ What's the smallest version of this that's still great?
◈ What's the part that might disappoint people?
◈ What did you consider and throw out?
◈ If this fails, why will it fail?

Here's how you can apply the Dear Customer Letter, whether you're launching the next big thing or refining a product that's been around for years.

SPEAK TO YOUR CUSTOMER, NOT AT THEM

The heart of the Dear Customer Letter is its tone. You're not writing for stockholders or an industry blog; you're writing for the people who will actually use what you've built. Whether you're a startup introducing a breakthrough app or a legacy business launching a refined product, talk directly to your customers. Keep it simple, clear, and authentic. They don't need to know the intricacies of your internal processes—they care about how this new thing will make their lives better. Keep it personal, like a letter from an old friend.

MAKE IT ABOUT THEM, NOT YOU

Your letter is not an ego trip. It's about how your new service, product, or feature will solve a problem your customers face or bring them joy in ways they didn't expect. Too often, businesses fall into the trap of patting themselves on the back for their innovation. But the customer doesn't care about the shiny tech behind it—they care about how it makes their life easier, faster, or more enjoyable. In a startup, this might be a product that eliminates a pain point they didn't even realize was holding them back. In an established business, it might be an enhancement that streamlines an existing process. Either way, make it about them.

SHARE THE "HOW" IN A WAY THEY'LL GET

Once you've captured their interest, walk them through how it works. But remember: your customer doesn't speak your internal language, so don't drown them in technical details. Instead, paint a picture of the customer experience in everyday terms. If you're a startup, take them through how to interact with your product, step by step. If you're an established business, focus on how the improvement changes the way they use what they already know and love. Make it simple, relatable, and, above all, easy to visualize.

A CALL TO ACTION THAT MATTERS

The final push in your letter isn't just a sign-off—it's a direct invitation for the customer to engage. Tell them what to do next, whether it's clicking a link, signing up, or trying out your new feature. And don't be coy—make it as frictionless as possible. In startups, the urgency might be higher, pushing for early adoption. In established companies, it's about ensuring customers know where to find the value in the sea of existing offerings. Guide them straight to the good stuff.

GRATITUDE THAT'S REAL

End with thanks—genuine, unforced, and heartfelt. Customers have options, and they've chosen you. Whether you're fighting for market share as a new player or holding onto loyal customers as a longstanding brand, gratitude is always in style. But this isn't just a formality. It's a reminder that without them, there's no you. The best businesses—whether emerging or established—never lose sight of that simple truth.

REAL WORLD EXAMPLE OF THE AMAZON PRESS RELEASE

This method was used to get support for this program, which was the Launchpad Innovation Grants applying the exact method, with a real Amazon press release to reference. I've written a plethora of these internally, and this is the best one I can reference since it's public record.

At first, nobody wanted this program. Not the execs. Not the teams. It was another idea on a long list of "maybe someday" projects that never see daylight. Too complicated, too risky, too much effort for an unclear return. But the thing about resistance? It usually means you're onto something.

The trick was getting people to see the opportunity hiding in plain sight.

STEP 1: LISTEN—FIND THE REAL PROBLEM

Australian small businesses weren't just struggling; they were adapting. They didn't need sympathy—they needed tools, reach, and a way to turn survival into scale. The data showed it: 89% felt more resilient, 92% were optimistic, and 78% had turned to e-commerce to stay alive. But what they lacked? Visibility, marketing power, and an actual shot at competing.

STEP 2: DEFINE—CUT THROUGH THE NOISE

This wasn't about handing out free money to SMBs and calling it a day. The real issue wasn't just financial—it was about exposure. Small businesses needed a way to get in front of customers who didn't know they existed. Amazon needed new selection, new sellers, and fresh blood in the ecosystem.

The challenge? Prove that this wasn't charity. It was strategy. If small businesses grew, Amazon grew. More sellers meant more selection. More selection meant more customers. More customers meant more revenue.

STEP 3: INVENT—BUILD SOMETHING THAT WORKS

So we built the Amazon Launchpad Innovation Grants. Not just a check, but a full-on rocket boost:

◈ **$20,000 cash** to fuel growth.
◈ **Amazon advertising support** to put winners in front of actual buyers.
◈ **A bootcamp with Amazon experts**—because knowledge beats luck.
◈ **A national ad package** to push winners into the mainstream.
◈ **Mentorship and on-site marketing**—real, tangible levers for success.

Then, we added the twist: **a live pitch session to Amazon HQ.** Ten finalists, one shot, judged by industry leaders who know what it takes to make it. It turned an application into a high-stakes event, and suddenly, people started paying attention.

STEP 4: REFINE—MAKE IT BULLETPROOF

One iteration wasn't enough. We looked at what worked, what didn't, and tightened the screws. We pulled in past winners to prove impact. We refined the messaging—not just about helping small businesses but about bringing **new customers and new selection** to Amazon. That was the KPI that mattered.

STEP 5: TEST, FAIL, IMPROVE, WIN

Nobody wanted this program at first. But once we showed how it drove value—for sellers, for customers, for Amazon itself—the tune changed. Now, it's a full-fledged machine. Businesses apply. Customers get new products. Amazon gets fresh inventory and new sellers hungry to grow.

It started as an idea nobody wanted. It became an initiative nobody could ignore. That's how you get buy-in. That's how you make something real. For reference, here is the Amazon press release.

AMAZON LAUNCHPAD OFFERS AUSTRALIAN SMBS AN OPPORTUNITY TO PITCH TO AMAZON AU HQ FOR AN INNOVATION GRANT

New research reveals more than three-quarters (78%) of Australian SMBs will use e-commerce and digital tools to allow them to work from anywhere.

SYDNEY – 30 March 2021 – Twelve months on from the first lockdown restrictions across Australia, local SMBs are feeling resilient and optimistic, according to new research from Amazon Launchpad - Amazon.com.au's program to help Aussie startups and entrepreneurs bring innovative products to shoppers.

The research reveals that 89% of SMBs are feeling more resilient in running their businesses, 92% feel optimistic for the year ahead, and 78% of SMBs will use e-commerce and digital tools to allow them to work from anywhere.

Commissioned by Amazon Australia, the 2021 Amazon Launchpad Innovation Report explores the current sentiment amongst Australian SMB owners, how they've evolved their businesses over the past twelve months, and a look toward the year ahead.

To celebrate innovation by Australian startups, entrepreneurs, and SMBs as our way of life continues to change, Amazon Launchpad has today also announced that applications are open for its 2021 Innovation Grants initiative.

Chadd Ciccarelli, Head of Launchpad at Amazon

Australia said, "Lockdown restrictions have fast-tracked the digitalisation of Australian businesses with over three-quarters of SMBs saying e-commerce and digital tools have allowed them to run their business from anywhere."

"Amazon Launchpad is a unique program that helps start-ups and entrepreneurs reach their online potential, whether they live in Broken Hill, Tassie, or Far North Queensland. We hope that this year's Innovation Grants will nurture the ingenuity that Aussie entrepreneurs are famous for and help the winners grow their businesses through e-commerce."

This year's five Innovation grant packages are worth more than $200,000 each and include: a $20,000 cash grant, Amazon advertising support, an exclusive boot camp experience with access to Amazon experts, a national advertising package with JCDecaux Nurture, industry mentorship, and onsite marketing placements on Amazon. com.au.

In a twist to this year's initiative, Amazon Launchpad will give ten finalists the opportunity to virtually pitch their entry direct into Amazon Australia HQ, to a panel of judges. This year's judges are Chadd Ciccarelli from

Amazon Launchpad, last year's grant recipients Rosa-Clare Willis and Andrew Ford from Crockd; Carolyn Creswell, founder of the country's leading muesli brand, Carman's, and managing partner, Kylie Frazer, of tech investment group, Eleanor Ventures.

2020 Amazon Launchpad grant winner and 2021 judge, Rosa-Clare Willis of DIY Pottery Kit brand, Crockd, said, "Not only did Amazon Launchpad open our eyes to Amazon as a marketing and distribution channel, but the program provided the support we needed during 2020. The mentorship we've received has been incredible, and we're seeing our business grow on Amazon.com.au.

"You've got to be in it to win it, and to any small business out there, who's wondering whether they should apply for a grant, I say, you've got nothing to lose and everything to gain!"

Other key 2021 Amazon Launchpad Innovation Report findings:

◈ The e-commerce opportunity: more than a third (39%) of SMBs said their customers are more open to buying online now than 12 months ago, four in ten (41%) have seen an increase in online enquiries about their business over the past 12 months, and one in six (15%) of SMBs made a sale online for the first time ever in the past year.

◈ It's all about innovation: to help navigate the uncertainty of the past twelve months, almost a third (30%) of SMBs said they invested in product or business innovation to reach new customers, and 82% said they will lean into innovation to grow their business over the next 12 months.

◈ Top areas businesses are innovating in this year: growing their digital presence (42%), taking their business into new markets (39%), and revising product offering (33%).

◈ Digital tools empower businesses for growth: four-fifths (81%) of SMBs will use digital tools to network over the next 12 months, and more than two-thirds (69%) will use online channels to seek investment in their business.

◈ What Aussie SMBs need most in 2021: businesses have rated access to new customers (47%) and support with marketing, advertising, and social media activity (34%) over financial support (31%). Additionally, almost a third (30%) said they need help with future growth planning and innovation.

The Amazon Launchpad Innovation Grants entry period is from today to 11:59 p.m. AEST, 10 May on www. Amazon.com.au/Launchpad.

The five Amazon Launchpad grant recipients from across Australia will be publicly announced in June 2021.

FINAL THOUGHT: IT'S ALL TRASH UNTIL IT'S CASH

If you've made it this far, you already know the truth: No one gives a damn about your ideas. They care about what works. They care about results. They care about things that make their lives better, easier, or more interesting. Everything else? Noise. Background static in a world already drowning in half-baked dreams and startup graveyards.

Amazon didn't become the behemoth it is because of brilliant ideas alone. It got there through relentless execution, brutal prioritization, and an obsession with what customers actually want. And that's the lesson that cuts across every strategy, every leadership principle, every battle-tested framework in this book. Execution is king.

César Gueikian, President and CEO of Gibson Brands, put it simply: "DO EPIC SHIT!" Not safe shit. Not comfortable shit. Not "let's see what happens" shit. Epic. That means testing, failing, learning, and doing it all over again until you carve something out that sticks. It means stripping away the fluff, the ego, and the unnecessary complexity until all that's left is something undeniable—something people will pay for, fight for, and talk about.

Throughout this book, we've pulled apart Amazon's playbook to uncover what actually works:

◈ **Leadership Principles** aren't just words—they're a system for driving results, earning trust, and building a culture of ownership.

- ❖ **The STAR Method** isn't just an interview trick—it's how you separate A-players from dead weight and build a team that actually delivers.
- ❖ **The Working Backwards Process** isn't some corporate exercise—it's the fastest way to filter out bullshit and ensure you're building something people want.
- ❖ **Navigating toxic environments** isn't about playing politics—it's about knowing when to fight, when to walk away, and how to keep your integrity intact while still winning.
- ❖ **Building something that lasts** isn't about hype—it's about solving real problems, creating value, and making sure your work stands the test of time.

None of this is theoretical. It's what works. It's what separates the dreamers from the doers. The people who make noise from the people who make money. The ones who build something real from the ones who sit around talking about it.

So here's the bottom line: Stop waiting for permission. Stop waiting for perfect conditions. Stop worrying about whether your idea is good enough. Get out there, start testing, take the hits, and refine until you get it right. Because everything is trash until someone proves it's worth cash.

This isn't the end. It's the starting line. Now go build something that matters.